D1458380

An extraordinary gathering of

Angels

An extraordinary gathering of
Angels
MARGARET BARKER

previous page: Mary, Queen of Heaven (angel detail), Master of the St. Lucy Legend, late 15th century, Flemish

pages 8–9: Choir of Angels, mosaic apse of the Church of St. Paolo entro le Mura, Rome, Edward Burne-Jones, 1872–76, English

If you wish to display the movement of an angel,
Why, painter, do you paint this winged man,
And not intelligence, spirit, light and flame?
Only one could not paint the immaterial with what
is material.

MANUEL PHILES

This book is dedicated to my grandson, James William Barker.

An extraordinary gathering of angels has made this book possible, and I should like to thank them all: first my husband and family, and then the staff at MQ Publications, especially Ljiljana Baird and Leon Meyer.

I am very grateful to all who contributed the interviews, which have broadened the scope of this book, and to those who sent me pictures and references, answered my questions, located texts, took photos, lent me books or helped in many other ways: Bishop Basil, Bruce Clark, John Drackley, Paul Gikas, Wendy Hancock, Douglas Hedley, Pat Kelvie, Yuri Klitchenko, Tom O'Loughlin, Ronald and Anne Loxley, David Melling, David Miles, Robert Murray, Graham Randles, Jessica Rose, Michael and Anne Osborne, Peter Shelton, Abbot Silouan, Thomas Small, and Alan Stott.

The angels too have helped produce this book. Nothing else could explain the extraordinary way in which information seemed to materialize from the most unlikely sources. There is no such thing as coincidence, especially when writing about angels.

MARGARET BARKER, 2004

The Angel Raphael Leaving Tobit and his Family (detail), Rembrandt, c. 1637, Dutch

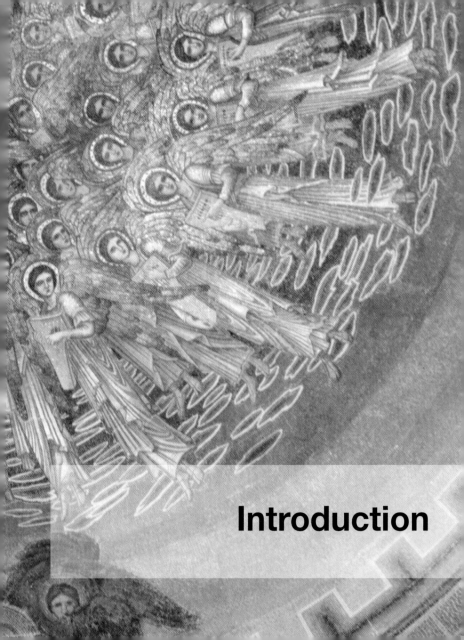

Introduction

The Unseen World

Angels are unseen forces in the creation. They connect the material world of our everyday lives to the Source of all life whom we call God. They are the means by which we can know something of God, and the only means by which we can have complete knowledge of the creation. They reveal what human minds could not work out for themselves, and they are also guides along the many paths of human reasoning.

"Angel" means messenger, and humans experience angels primarily as messengers. But this is not what they "are;" this is what they do. Angels exist to praise God, and humans who experience their presence are being guided toward this universal hymn of praise. Mystics and seers have heard their song, and those who respond to the angels' message move inevitably toward the harmony the angels represent, the "peace on earth" of the Bethlehem angels. By joining the song of the angels, human hearts and minds are connected to the power of the invisible creation, and their lives are renewed.

The Bible pictures creation as a state of two parts: the visible and the invisible, and so Christians declare their belief in One God, the Father Almighty, Maker of heaven and earth and of "all things visible and invisible."[1] They believe that life without the angels is not a liberation but an unnatural state, impoverished because cut off from the power of the angels and diminished by loss of the greater reality that is just beyond our rational perception.

right: **Baptism of Christ (detail), Orazio Gentileschi, 1603, Italian**
Ezekiel described the "gleaming bronze" appearance of the angel who carried him through the air to Jerusalem. Sometimes the Hebrew word used is translated "the color of amber."

THE HOLY OF HOLIES, IN   THE TEMPLE OF SOLOMON

The Ark of ÿ Covenant, shewing
ÿ barrs on ÿ sides [1 K. VIII. 8]. The
Cherubims above on ÿ covenant
each with two wings without
hands, and a Cloud above be-

-tween ÿ Cherubims, which seems
to shine, and to be, as it were, em-
braced by the wings of the
Cherubims. according to
Schaccus, & others.

2

The Temple

The temple of King Solomon in Jerusalem, completed in about 960 B.C.E., depicted the whole creation, and was the larger, permanent version of the tabernacle or tent that Moses had constructed in the desert. It was divided in two by a curtain, to show that there were two parts to the creation and that the world of God and the angels was always present but hidden from human eyes.

The outer part of the temple was "the holy place," meaning that it had been made holy, and it represented the visible world of ordinary human life. The sanctuary beyond the curtain, however, was the invisible world of the angels. This was called the "most holy place," meaning that it was the source of the holiness that made the rest of creation holy. It was the presence of God. The world of human life could only receive holiness, life, and power as gifts from the presence of God, and angels were the messengers who brought those gifts.

The temple pattern of creation is set out in Genesis 1, when the Hebrew storyteller describes how the world was created in six days. Jewish tradition said the six days represented the stages of building the tabernacle. On Day One there was light, separated from darkness, and this corresponded to the holy of holies. This light was the presence of God and the state of the angels, who were both in the light and of the light. Just as light cannot be divided into distinct parts, but is all one, so too the angels of Day One are in some sense one.

left: **Interior of the Holy of Holies in Solomon's Temple, from *In Ezechielum Explanations*, Juan Bautista Villalpando, 1594–1605, Spanish**
The prophet Ezekiel described the temple as a place of angels. The walls were decorated with palm trees and cherubim, four-winged heavenly creatures with bovine feet. In the midst of the cherubim is the ark.

On the second day the firmament, represented by the veil, separated the upper world of the angels from the lower world of mortals; and on subsequent days the visible world came into being: dry land and vegetation, and the creatures of sea, air, and land. The veil marked the division between the visible and the invisible creation. It represented matter, and was woven from red, blue, purple, and white threads, to represent the four elements from which the material world was made: earth (white), air (blue), fire (red), and water (purple). It was embroidered with cherubim, the winged heavenly beings found throughout the temple—in the holy of holies, on the walls of the great hall, and on the veil between them. They could move between the two states of creation, and transmitted heavenly knowledge to earth.

When priests in the great hall looked toward the holy of holies and saw the cherubim on the veil, they glimpsed what lay beyond the veil. The icon screen in an Orthodox church, with its pictures of saints and angels, is set in a similar position and has a similar role. It is the boundary between the part of the church that represents heaven and the part that represents earth, and the saints and angels afford a glimpse of heaven to those still on earth. They are windows into heaven.

right: **The Seven Angels with the Harps of God (detail), the Apocalypse of Angers tapestry, Nicholas Bataille, 1375–78, Flemish**
The veil of the temple was woven with "skilled work," presumably a form of tapestry, depicting cherubim.

Time and Eternity

The veil also separated time from the state beyond time. In the temple, eternity did not mean a long period of time, but a state without time, and the angels passed between time and eternity. Mystics and other people of genius often describe the timeless moment or the dream experience when something new was revealed to them.

Time and matter are how we distinguish one thing from another, or one event from another. If there is neither matter nor time, there is nothing to divide or be divided. In the Genesis creation story, this state is called Day One, the state of original unity. Those who entered it saw the unity of all things, without the divisions and distinctions that characterize the visible state.

They saw the unity of the material creation and the totality of time, and so prophets could describe what was yet to come. Time was not linear or cyclic but rooted in the veiled present of eternity. In the timeless state, knowledge is not "acquired" since this would involve time, nor does that knowledge change. Modern cosmologists are discovering new dimensions to the "scientific" concept of time, and they are remarkably like those of the angels. "To know timelessly must therefore involve knowing all events throughout time."[2]

right: **Last Judgement (detail, Paradise), Fra Angelico, 1432–35, Italian**
When the Son of Man returns to judge the earth, he will divide the nations as a shepherd divides sheep from goats. The blessed he will set at his right hand and allow to enter the Kingdom. They will join the angels in Paradise.

Perceiving Angels

Angels can be perceived by any of the human senses, but only when they enter our state of time and matter are they perceived as distinct beings. A recent survey showed that most people who experienced an angel had not seen anything, but there are practical difficulties in conveying a sense of perfume or ethereal sound, a warm enfolding presence, a particular taste sensation, or a moment of spiritual or intellectual illumination. The most familiar angels are therefore those in pictures. Even when the angel story does not say the angel was visible, artists have added a winged figure. When Gabriel spoke to Mary, St. Luke did not say that the angel was seen. Mary only heard his words. The Bible has many accounts of angels being perceived but not seen.

The perfume of angels is described in various ways: the scent of flowers, perhaps, or sweet myrrh. When Solomon's temple was consecrated, the fragrance showed that God was dwelling there.[3] A Christian priest would touch the ears and nostrils of those he baptized, so that the holy of holies opened for them and they entered the place where life was renewed.[4] In other words, they could perceive the angels, and begin to live as angels, albeit in the material world. They were able to transmit angel fragrance and knowledge throughout the visible creation. St. Paul said that Christians spread the fragrance of Christ's knowledge, because they were themselves that sweet perfume.[5]

left: Madonna and Child enthroned with Saints (detail), Domenico Ghirlandaio, c. 1486, Italian
Angels are beings beyond time and space. They have no obvious age or gender.

Knowledge of Angels

There can be no objective knowledge of angels, no glimpse of the state beyond the veil that is just intellectual enquiry. Knowledge of the angels, both knowing angels and knowing what they know, is knowledge of a different order. It is beyond human knowledge, and once received, supersedes all human knowledge. It cannot be unlearned; there is no going back. Enigmatic lines in the Old Testament seem to describe a man who has no wisdom or knowledge of the holy ones, because he has not been into heaven.[6]

The heavenly knowledge was known as Wisdom, and it transformed people. Enoch, one of the key figures in the Jewish and Christian angel traditions, described the ritual for consecrating a high priest. He said that when he stood before the throne in the holy of holies, he was transformed into an angel: taken out of his material body, clothed with a garment of the Lord's glory and anointed with sweet myrrh oil. When he had been united with the Glory, an archangel taught him all the secrets of the creation, and he then returned to the material world as an angel, a messenger.[7]

Anyone who experiences the angel presence is changed by it and becomes, in a very real sense, part of it. S/he becomes wise, another angel and part of that unity which is the Source of life. The knowledge angels bring cannot be distinguished from this sense of love and unity.

Christians believe that the complete "fullness" of the divine state was present in Christ, and so he could hold together all things, and

right: **Angel, Abbot Handerson Thayer, 1889, American**
Some angels are described as "men in white," because they wear white linen garments. White linen fabric was a symbol of immortality, in contrast to white wool which came from an animal that would die.

reconcile all divisions.[9] St. Paul wrote of people rooted and grounded in love, able to comprehend the breadth, length, height, and depth, to know Christ's love which surpasses all knowledge, and be filled with the "fullness of God."[10] This is the angel state, being caught up into the light and fragrance, becoming part of it. Such people—the saints—have a halo to show they brought some divine light into the material creation. People often sensed an inexplicable fragrance in their presence. In one sense all Christians have halos, because all are saints. Paul wrote to "the saints" in this city or that,[11] and "the communion of saints" is part of the Apostles' Creed.

Poets and artists continue to have a place for the angels, and Christian prayers—even modern, revised, and up-to-date prayers—still speak of them. But theologians are often wary. Martin Israel, in his book *Angels, Messengers of Grace* wrote this: "Younger priests, familiar with depth psychology (to say nothing of computer science and its challenge of artificial intelligence) will shake their heads impatiently at the repetition of such nonsense, unless personal experience suddenly opens their closed minds to areas of life that were previously hidden from view. This closure of the mind is the result of pride, (the attitude that modern humans know it all), ignorance, and a vague, scarcely formulated, fear of the unknown."[13]

above: **Tahitian Nativity, Paul Gauguin, 1896, French**

Angels know no boundaries of time or place. Here, a mother and her child in Tahiti are at the eternal Nativity with a watching angel.

Interview with Bishop Basil of Sergievo
Russian Orthodox Church

What is the role of the angels in the life of an Orthodox Christian?

For an Orthodox Christian the heart of his or her life in the Church is the Divine Liturgy, and it is through the Liturgy and through prayer that we become aware of the presence of angels and their role in the creation. The Eucharistic Liturgy itself is accompanied by angels, and the Archangels Michael and Gabriel often figure prominently on the icon screen of an Orthodox church, generally on the north and south doors, as messengers between the visible and invisible worlds. During the Entrance with Gospel, the priests pray "that with our entrance there may be an entrance of holy angels, ministering with us and with us glorifying thy goodness." Then at the Great Entrance with the Holy Gifts of bread and wine, the people sing: "We who in a mystery represent the cherubim and sing the thrice holy hymn to the life-giving Trinity, let us now lay aside every care of this life … that we may receive the King of all, invisible escorted by hosts of angels." The entire liturgy is celebrated by the gathered community, with and among the angels. And, of course, there is the often repeated petition by the deacon asking that God may give each of us "an angel of peace, a faithful guide, a guardian of our souls and bodies."

The angels are, for an Orthodox Christian, a host of invisible powers present throughout the creation, mediating to us the providential goodness and power of God. They join us in our worship—or rather, we join them in their worship, thereby linking our prayer with the prayer of the earliest Christians and with the worship of the temple in Jerusalem.

God himself, "borne on the throne of the cherubim, the Lord of the Seraphim," "is at rest amidst the holy ones [the angels]," and it is "with these blessed powers … [that] we also cry aloud and say: Holy art thou and all holy, thou and thine only begotten Son and thy Holy Spirit." The role of the angels is to bind this visible world—and us with it—to God.

NOTES

1 THE NICENE CREED. **2** PAUL DAVIES GOD AND THE NEW PHYSICS, P. 134. **3** JOSEPHUS, ANTIQUITIES 8.4. **4** AMBROSE ON THE MYSTERIES 1.3; 2.5. **5** 2 CORINTHIANS 2.14-5. **6** PROVERBS 30.3-4. **7** 2 ENOCH 22. **8** GENESIS 4.1. **9** COLOSSIANS 1.17-20. **10** EPHESIANS 3.17-19. **11** E.G. 1 CORINTHIANS 1.2; PHILIPPIANS 1.1. **12** CLOUD OF UNKNOWING, CHAPTER 6. **13** LONDON: SPCK 1995, P.51.

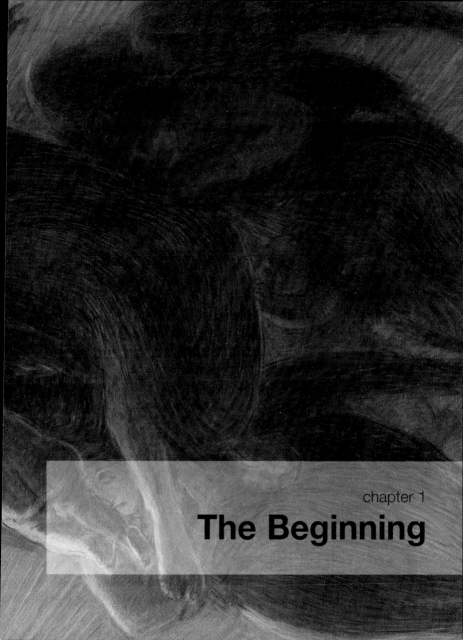

chapter 1
The Beginning

The Source of Life

St. John saw the Source of all life in the holy of holies. When he saw the throne of God, he was looking into the heart of creation. The Dead Sea Scrolls called this the "mystery of becoming," and those who saw it knew "the paths of everything that lives."[1] The pattern of the angels was the pattern for all things in the visible creation, and so knowing the angels was essential for understanding the material world.

St. John heard the angel song, praising the Lord as the One who continually creates and holds all things in existence. That is what the name Yahweh (the Lord) means. The song of the heavenly host proclaims and sustains the harmony of creation.

Worthy art thou, our Lord and God,
to receive Glory and honour and power,
for thou didst create all things,
and by thy will they existed and were created.[2]

previous page: **Creation of Light, Gaetano Previati, late 19th century, Italian**
In the beginning, God called the light into being, and the angels were part of that light. We see the light of Day One when we meet an angel.

left: **Creation of the World, fresco in the dome of the Baptistery, Padua Cathedral, Giusto de Menabuoi, 1375–78, Italian**
St. John's Gospel opens by saying that the Word was in the beginning with God, and here, the cross in his halo shows that the Creator is the Second Person of the Trinity.

Visions in the Holy of Holies

The visions of Enoch record what he saw in the holy of holies. An angel showed him the heart of the creation, all the secrets and mysteries of natural phenomena, and how the unity, here called the kingdom, is divided to become the visible creation. He saw how the winds and weathers originated; he saw the paths of the sun, moon, and stars, and how they were kept in balance by a great oath or bond.[3] Each was an angel, whom the Creator called by name. Enoch was told by his angel guide that he would learn all the secret things around the Lord of Spirits,[4] and later he saw how all these natural phenomena related to each other; how thunder related to lightning, for example, and why there was a time lapse between the two, how clouds and mist are related, and how the rain-bearing winds come into being.[5]

The Aramaic fragments of 1 Enoch found among the Dead Sea Scrolls, preserve the oldest lists of angel names. The fallen angels had such names as Kokab'el, meaning star of God, Ra'm'el, meaning Thunder of God, Baraq'el, meaning Lightning of God, Matar'el, meaning Rain of God, Shamshiel, meaning sun of God, and 'Anan'el meaning cloud of God. In each case, the fallen angel revealed the knowledge implied by his name: Kokab'el taught about the stars and Shamshiel about the sun. The Sacred Name of the greatest angel was Yahweh (the Lord) and it meant "causing to be." The Lord created life.

Each of what we should call natural phenomena was an angel, praising the Creator and bound by his bond.[6] Evil angels tried to learn the Sacred Name, which was the secret of the great bond, so that they too could create. They did not succeed, and so never discovered how earth and heaven kept their place, how the sea knew its limits, how the sun, moon, and stars stayed in their courses and made possible a calendar. Enoch's description of the angels, and how they related to each other, was the natural science of his time, and the angel lore was a deposit of scientific knowledge.

Enoch saw not only the angels of creation, but also how they were agents of the Lord's judgment on those who did not acknowledge the Lord of Spirits, that is, those who denied the Creator and the angels he caused to be. The angel system described by Enoch recognized that human conduct was a part of the Creator's system, and so conduct that ignored his Law impacted on the whole creation. Those who did not humbly acknowledge the Source of all power would be destroyed and their works would vanish.[7]

The Lord reminded Job that he did not have this angel knowledge. He had not seen the origin of the creation and so he could not understand it. He had not been present when the foundations of the earth were set in place, when the angels sang as the creation came into existence.[8] He knew nothing of the winds and rain, the clouds and lightning[9]—in other words, he knew nothing about the hidden angels. He did not even know about the visible creation, the life of wild animals and birds, and if he did not understand the creation, how could he understand the ways of God?[10]

Much of this angel lore does not appear in the Hebrew Bible, since it concerned the holy of holies, which was the exclusive preserve of the high priests.[11] Ordinary people were warned that the secret things belonged to the Lord, and that their duty was simply to obey the revealed commandments.[12] No angels are mentioned on Day One of the Genesis creation story, because this biblical account tells only of the visible creation. They do, however, appear in the summary at the end: "Thus the heavens and the earth were finished, and all the host of them."[13]

For on the first day he created the heavens, which are above, and the earth, and the waters and all the spirits which minister before him:

The angels of the presence
The angels of sanctification
The angels of the spirit of fire
The angels of the spirit of the winds
The angels of the spirit of the clouds and darkness and snow and hail and frost,
The angels of the resoundings and thunder and lightning
The angels of the spirits of cold and heat and winter and springtime and harvest and summer
And all of the spirits of his creatures which are in heaven and on earth.

BOOK OF JUBILEES 2.2

right: **The Creation, engraving, Jacobus van de Schley, 18th century, Dutch**
Even though the Genesis creation story does not mention any angels, Psalm 104 and the Benedicite imply that there were angels on Day One, and the Book of Jubilees lists their ranks.

following page: **Creation of Man, detail from the Dome of the Creation, St. Mark's Basilica, Venice, early 13th century**
In this series of scenes, each of the days of creation has its own angel. By the sixth day, God is accompanied by six angels.

No clouds gathered in the skies and the polluted streams became clear, whilst celestial music rang through the air and the angels rejoiced with gladness. With no selfish or partial joy but for the sake of the law they rejoiced, for creation engulfed in the ocean of pain was now to obtain release.

GAUTAMA BUDDHA

left: **Angel sundial on Chartres Cathedral, France, 1578**
The Enoch astronomy book shows that angels revealed how to measure time and calculate a calendar. The angels stand, literally, behind time.

following page left: **Phases of the Moon, from "The Celestial Atlas, or The Harmony of the Universe," Andreas Cellarius, 1660–61, Dutch**
The angels were believed to be the principles of the universe. Since the angels were all part of the divine Unity, the creation was also one great system.

following page right: **The Four Angels holding the Winds, from the Apocalypse of St. John, 13th century, English or French**
Angels are invisible forces in the creation, associated with natural phenomena. Here, they are set at the four corners of the world, limiting the power of the winds.

The Unity of the Angels

The angels are the unity of Day One but in our material world we perceive them as separate beings. There are many ranks of angels, but all are part of the One. A Gnostic text of the second century C.E. found in Egypt compares the heavenly beings to units of time. Just as all units of time—hours, months, and years—are parts of the greater whole, so too the individual angels we perceive are part of the greater unity.[14] Another text explains that the angels began as a unity, and Jesus came from the state of unity in order to reunite separated human beings to the angels and thus to the One.[15]

One name for angels in the Hebrew Scriptures is *'elohim*, a word that is plural in form, but usually understood as singular. "God" and the unity of *'elohim* was emphasized. The most important statement in the Hebrew Scriptures is "The Lord our *'elohim*, the Lord is One."[16]

Josephus, who was a younger contemporary of Jesus, must have understood the Lord as a cluster of angels. When he retold the story of the Lord appearing with two angels at Mamre, he did not mention the Lord. He spoke only of three angels.[17] Thus, too, the traditional Jewish commentary on this passage: Abraham saw the three archangels Michael, Gabriel and Raphael, and the Lord is not mentioned.[18] They must have believed that the Lord himself was present in his angels. Philo, another contemporary of Jesus, described the Lord as the First Angel, the Logos, but the other angels were Logoi, the plural of Logos.[19]

Jesus prayed that his disciples would be one, like the angels. Their unity would be the proof that Jesus was from the One. He used the image of the holy of holies, and of the Glory he had shared in that state before the world had been created. He had passed the Glory on to his disciples, so they too would bring the Glory into the visible creation.[20]

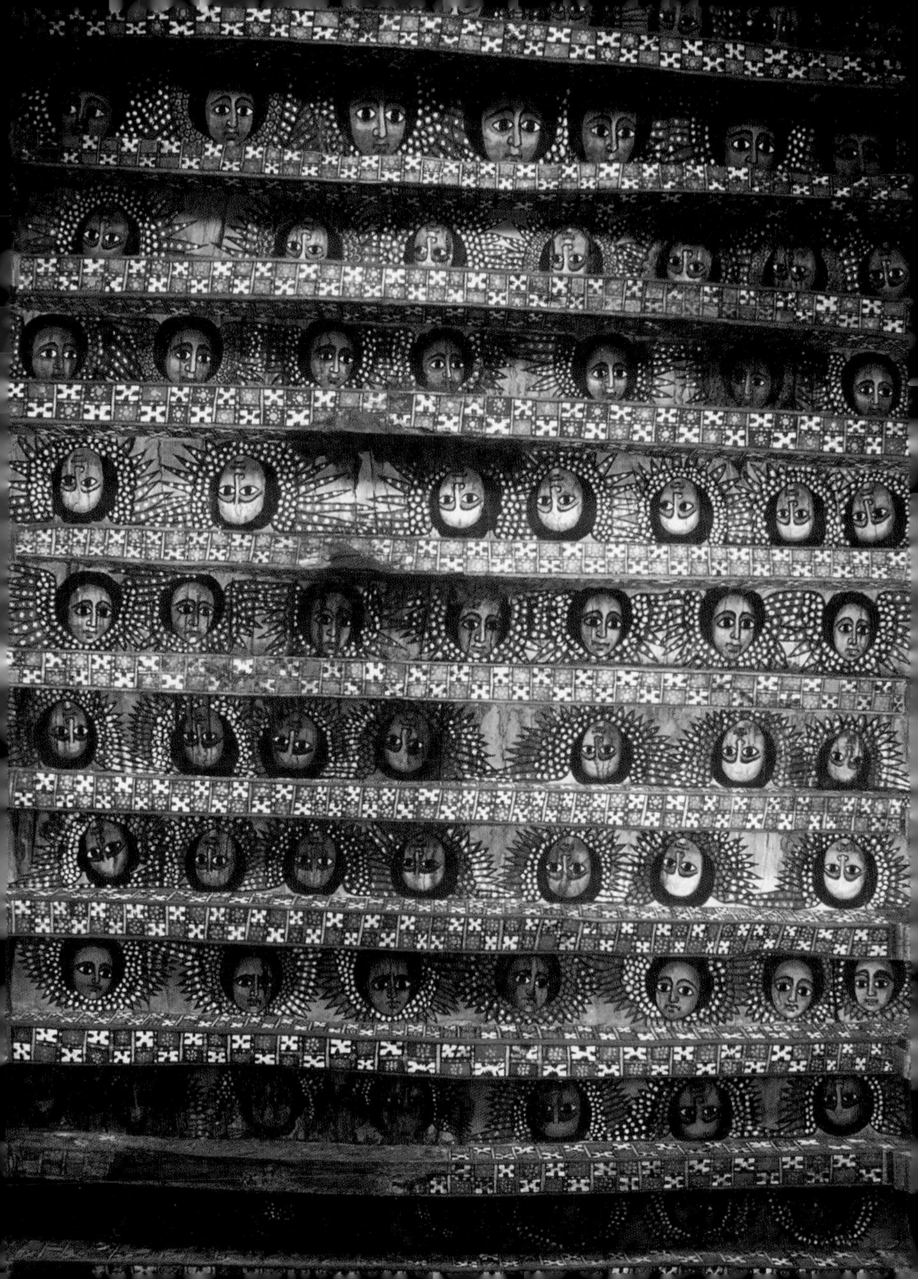

Becoming an Angel

People can become angels. The process is called resurrection. Jesus himself said that angels are sons of God and sons of resurrection,[21] and so people who experience resurrection become angels. Resurrection, however, does not only occur after physical death. It occurs when one enters the presence of God and glimpses the Glory, and so Enoch was resurrected when he stood before the Lord and became one of the glorious ones. This must have been what St. Philip meant when he asked Jesus to show him the Father, and Jesus replied "He who has seen me has seen the Father."[22] "We," said St. John, "have beheld his Glory,"[23] and so have become angels on earth.

St. Paul wrote to the Christians at Colossae that they had already been resurrected, and so should have the lifestyle of heaven and not of this earth.[24] He addressed them as saints, that is, holy ones, and spoke to them as the angels who lived in Colossae.[25] Baptism was the moment when Christians believed they were resurrected, and so as they came up from the water, they put on white robes to show they had become angels.

Since the home of the angels was the Unity of the Holy of Holies, St. John saw the heavenly city as a golden cube, a holy of holies. It needed no sun or moon; it was lit by the Glory of the presence of God. He saw too the river of life flowing through the city, and the tree of life whose leaves would heal the nations. Enoch called this place the undivided kingdom. Jesus called it the Kingdom of God.

previous page: **The painted ceiling of the Church of Debre Birhan Selassie, Ethiopia, 17th century**
Ceilings such as this remind us that the whole creation is suffused with angels and is in their care.

above: **The Spirits' Flight, 19th century illustration, British**

St. Paul told the Christians in Colossae to set their minds on the things above,
because they were already resurrected with Christ.

Interview with Professor Dr. Bernhard Lang

University of Paderborn, Germany

What did Emanuel Swedenborg believe about angels?

Swedenborg was a Swedish engineer, and one of the representatives of the pious Enlightenment. He believed that angels are our best friends in the universe.

Angels can—and indeed do—influence our feelings and emotional life to the extent that we are open to them and willing to let them do what God has assigned to them. Under angelic influence and inspiration, evil intentions may be removed and our will to do what is good and right may be strengthened, though angels never force us to do anything. Instead they give us a sense of strength and determination.

Swedenborg claims to have had more immediate mental contact with angels than most people; he believed, indeed, that he had been granted communication with angels almost daily for many years. What he learned he confided to his diaries, and from these he took material, which he eventually published in Latin.

In his books he explains that angels are not substantially different from human beings; rather, they are former humans, who, after shedding their earthly bodies in death, have been changed into spiritual beings. Although now living in spiritual worlds in splendid circumstances, they are not idle, for God assigns them many tasks. While some of their activities are carried out in other worlds, others are done in our human world and for our benefit.

One of Swedenborg's most daring and most famous teachings related to the social life of angelic beings. Angels, he taught, are not isolated beings that lose their appetite for communication and union with others. Living in societies, each is married to an angel of the opposite sex. Those men and women who truly love their spouse will be reunited with him or her in the afterlife, and so angelic marriage is for both time and eternity. Swedenborg sums up his teaching in the dictum: "We have been created to enter heaven and become angels."

NOTES

1 4Q 417.418. **2** REVELATION 4.11. **3** 1 ENOCH 41–43. **4** 1 ENOCH 52. **5** 1 ENOCH 60. **6** 1 ENOCH 69. **7** 1 ENOCH 69. **8** JOB 38.7. **9** JOB 38. **10** JOB 26.14. **11** NUMBERS 18.7. **12** DEUTERONOMY 29.29. **13** GENESIS 2.1. **14** EUGNOSTOS 84. **15** EXCERPTS FROM THEODOUS 36. **16** DEUTERONOMY 6.4. **17** JOSEPHUS, ANTIQUITIES 1.196. **18** GENESIS RABBAH L.2. **19** PHILO. TONGUES 146. **20** JOHN 17. **21** LUKE 20.36. **22** JOHN 14.9. **23** JOHN 1.14. **24** COLOSSIANS 3.1. **25** COLOSSIANS 1.2.

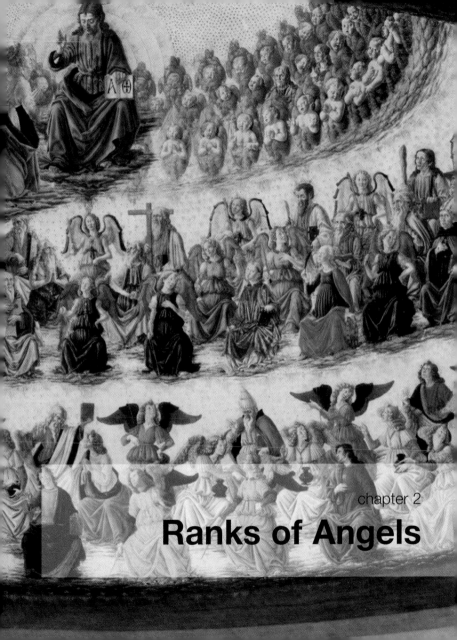

chapter 2

Ranks of Angels

Hosts of Heaven

There are many ranks in the hosts of heaven. The Old Testament mentions angels and archangels, cherubim and seraphim, holy ones and watchers, sons of God and princes. In the New Testament, St. Paul wrote of principalities, and powers, might and dominations,[1] and of thrones, dominations, principalities and powers.[2] Christ, who had been declared to be the Son, was above the angels.[3] St. John was warned not to worship angels, since both angels and mortals should unite in the worship of God,[4] and St. Paul also warned against angel worship.[5] Christ, he said, had triumphed over the principalities and powers,[6] showing that not all the heavenly beings were benign, and elsewhere he wrote of the spiritual hosts of wickedness in the heavenly places.[7]

The Nine Ranks of Angels

Pope St. Gregory the Great (died 604 C.E.) explained how there were nine orders of angels: the five mentioned by St. Paul—principalities, powers, virtues ("might"), dominations, and thrones—together with the angels and archangels, cherubim and seraphim. These had already been described in detail by St. Dionysius the Areopagite in about 500 C.E. The nine ranks are divided into three groups of three: highest, and therefore nearest to the throne of God, are seraphim, cherubim and thrones; lower are the dominations, virtues and powers; and in the lowest rank of all are principalities, archangels and angels.

The earliest Christian account of the angel hierarchy is found in the Testament of Adam, and was probably written before 400 C.E. The lowest rank are angels, each of whom cares for one person. Next are the archangels who care for the other living creatures. Third are the archons who control the weather; fourth the authorities who control the sun, moon, and stars; fifth are the powers who control the demons; and sixth the dominions who rule over earthly kingdoms and determine their fate. The three highest ranks stand before Jesus the enthroned Messiah singing "Holy, Holy, Holy." The thrones guard the entrance to the holy of holies, the cherubim carry the throne, and the seraphim, the highest rank, serve in the inner chamber.[8]

All the angels are messengers insofar as higher orders transmit light/love/knowledge to the lower, and so the hierarchy diffuses divine light through the whole creation, visible and invisible. Everything in the light becomes One, and this illumination is known as Transfiguration. The transfigured creation is the Kingdom of God. The purpose of the angels is to enable all beings to become more like God and to be united to God, and their various names indicate the manner in which they reflect the truth of God. As each person is drawn higher, so s/he becomes part of the divine work, and in turn reflects to those further down the scale. Some are purified and then in turn purify; some are illumined and then illumine; some are perfected and then make others perfect.

The *Celestial Hierarchy* of Dionysius, with its three ranks of three, was shaped by the ideas of Plotinus, a neo-Platonist mystic, but the various ranks are all known in Scripture. Christian worship did not really adopt Dionysius' scheme of the nine ranks, but kept to the older, biblical pattern. Nine ranks or choirs of angels do, however, appear in medieval western art.

previous page: **Assumption of the Virgin, Francesco Botticini, 1476, Italian**
The angels are divided into nine ranks: the highest ranks are the seraphim, traditionally red figures, the cherubim, blue figures, and the thrones, yellow figures; the middle ranks are the Dominions, Virtues and Powers; and the lowest ranks are the Principalities, Archangels, and Angels.

Rank on rank the host of heaven
    spreads its vanguard on the way
As the Light of light descendeth
    from the realms of endless day,
That the powers of hell may vanish
    as the darkness clears away.

At his feet the six winged seraph;
    cherubim with sleepless eye
Veil their faces to the Presence,
    as with ceaseless voice they cry—
Alleluia, alleluia, alleluia
    Lord Most High.

THE LITURGY OF ST. JAMES

right: **The Adoration of the Shepherds with Angels, Lorenzo Costa, c.1499, Italian**
The nine ranks of angels, linking heaven and earth, gather to celebrate with heavenly music the birth of the Christ.

And the angel said—"I have learned that every man lives not through care of himself, but by love..."

LEO TOLSTOY

left: **Angels holding souls (detail), from The Triumph of Death, fresco in the Campo Santo, Pisa, Italy, attributed to Francesco Traini, mid-14th century, Italian**
Painted after the horror of the Black Death, the Guardian Angel of each person who has died keeps that soul safe from attack by demons, and takes it to heaven.

following page: **Seven angels seated above the clouds, from the Revelation of St. John, Gondar, Ethiopian, 1732**
The Lord and his angels rode in storm clouds. Here, seven angels with their shepherd's crooks are traveling in a storm chariot and sending out lightning.

The three Divine are in this hierarchy,
First the Dominions, and the Virtues next;
And the third order is that of the Powers.
Then in the dances twain penultimate
The Principalities and Archangels wheel;
The last is wholly of angelic sports.
These orders upward all of them are gazing,
And downward so prevail, that unto God
They all attracted are and all attract.

DANTE ALIGHIERI, *PARADISO*

left: **Archangels flanked by seraphim and cherubim, the inner container of the Reliquary of the True Cross (The Limburg Reliquary), c. 965, Byzantine**

Ten angel figures and ten pairs of heavenly powers guarded the precious relic. There are two pairs of unnamed angels above the arms of a cross and three pairs below, each accompanied by two cherubim or seraphim. The lowest panel depicts four-headed cherubim, standing by fiery wheels and labeled *archai*, meaning principalities. The middle and upper panels depict seraphim, with six wings and only one face, labeled *exousiai*, meaning powers.

The Mystic Crucifixion, Sandro Botticelli, c. 1496, Italian

Against a background of the city of Florence being engulfed by apocalyptic destruction, the Angel slays the demon, whilst Mary Magdalen clings to the foot of the cross.

Thrones, detail of mosaics on the cupola of Florence Baptistery, 1270–1300, Italian

The thrones were the third rank of the angels, and in the Book of Revelation, the twenty four elders sit on thrones around the Lamb. They were also known as the wheels, ophannim, because they carried the heavenly chariot throne. Here they are holding an almond-shaped object that symbolizes the throne in Byzantine tradition.

Hark, a tumult on the mountains as a great
  multitude!
Hark, an uproar of kingdoms, of nations
  gathering together—
The Lord of hosts is mustering a host
for battle.

ISAIAH 13

left: **Heavenly Army (Principalities), Guariento di Arpo, c. 1330–78, Italian**
Angels, especially the powers, are often depicted as warriors. They are creatures
of fire, and here, like all angels, they travel in a cloud.

When a man sleeps, the body tells the
soul what it has done during the day,
the soul then reports it to the spirit,
the spirit to the angel, the angel to the
cherub, the cherub to the seraph who
then brings it before God.

LEVITICUS RABBAH 22

right: **Seraph, with six wings decorated with eye motifs, fresco from the
exterior of the Moldovita Monastery, Romania, c. 1537**
Isaiah described six-winged seraphim next to the heavenly throne. Their name
means "the burning ones." St. John says they were also the living creatures,
whose six wings were full of eyes. Sometimes a face is shown, as here, but
sometimes they are represented by a cluster of wings.

Angels in the Enoch Traditions

**Their faces were like the shining sun;
Their eyes were like burning lamps;
From their mouths fire was coming forth;
Their clothing was various singing;
Their wings were more glistering than gold;
Their hands were whiter than snow**

2 ENOCH 1

The early Jewish mystical texts, especially the writings known as 1 Enoch and 2 Enoch, have vivid descriptions of heaven. Enoch ascended to heaven in clouds, where he saw a house of flames and crystal, with fiery cherubim. There was an inner house of fire in which the Great Glory was enthroned with a vast throng of angels before him. None could enter the inner house except the most holy ones who stood near him.[9] In another vision, Enoch saw the holy sons of God walking on flames of fire. Then the archangel Michael took him up to a higher heaven, where he saw seraphim, cherubim, and ophanim ("wheels"), the unsleeping ones who guard the throne. Countless angels encircled the house, and the archangels Michael, Raphael, Gabriel, and Phanuel went in and out of the throne room.[10]

Traveling through the heavens with his angel guide, Enoch saw the fiery ones who could appear as men[11] and he saw an abyss of fire where the rebel angels were imprisoned.[12] He also learned the names and roles of the seven archangels, "the holy angels who watch": Uriel, in charge of the world and the underworld; Raphael, in charge of human spirits; Raguel, an avenging angel; Michael, in charge of good people and chaos; Saraqiel, in charge of sinful spirits; Gabriel, in charge of the cherubim, the serpents, and Paradise; and Remiel, who cares for the resurrected.[13]

The Parables of Enoch have even more detail, and show a sophisticated angel theology that must have been the background to St. John's visions in the Book of Revelation. In these three visions of the holy of holies, Enoch saw righteous angels praying for the people on earth and he joined with those who do not sleep as they sang: "Holy Holy Holy."[14] He asked his angel guide about the four "faces" near the throne, and learned that they were Michael, Raphael, Gabriel, and Phanuel. He saw the angels who keep the stars and the lightning on their appointed path,[15] and he learned from his angel guide about the secrets of the creation. He saw angels of vengeance preparing to punish wicked rulers, and the four archangels preparing an abyss of fire for the evil angels.[16] He saw the whole host of heaven: holy ones, cherubim, seraphim, ophannim, angels of power, angels of principalities, powers of the earth, powers of the waters, and the Chosen One (the Messiah); and they were praising the Lord in unison, in the spirit of faith, wisdom, patience, mercy, judgment, peace, and goodness.[17]

Elsewhere there are different accounts of the angels. Enoch saw two shining men clothed in song, who took him through the heavens on their wings.[18] He saw the angel guardians of the stars and the weathers, and he saw warrior angels singing.[19] He also noticed that the fifth heaven was silent, because it was the place of the fallen angels who did not praise God.[20] In the sixth heaven he saw the seven archangels who bring harmony to all existence in heaven and earth and maintain the sweet singing of praise, and in the seventh he saw the Lord enthroned.[21] In the great light there was a fiery army of archangels, bodiless powers, archangels, angels, and shining wheels; and in their midst, the cherubim and the six-winged seraphim who covered the throne.[22]

In another Enoch text, the angels, described as the heavenly household, are hostile to anyone trying to approach the throne. It is the picture of an imperial court, with seven concentric palaces and the throne in the midst, and angel guardians who cast down their crowns before the superior ranks. The lowest rank are angels, then the whirling ones, the living creatures, the cherubim, the wheels, the seraphim, the watchers, and the holy ones.[23] Above them all is the great Metatron, who sits enthroned and crowned at the entrance to the innermost palace. In his earthly life he had been Enoch the high priest, but was now transformed into the greatest angel and known as the little Yahweh. Here was a human being who had become divine.

NOTES

1 EPHESIANS 1.21. **2** COLOSSIANS 1.16. **3** HEBREWS 1.4. **4** REVELATION 19.10. **5** COLOSSIANS 2.18. **6** COLOSSIANS 2.15. **7** EPHESIANS 6.12. **8** TESTAMENT OF ADAM 4. **9** 1 ENOCH 14. **10** 1 ENOCH 71. **11** 1 ENOCH 17. **12** 1 ENOCH 18. **13** 1 ENOCH 20. **14** 1 ENOCH 39. **15** 1 ENOCH 43. **16** 1 ENOCH 53–4. **17** 1 ENOCH 61. **18** 2 ENOCH 1. **19** 2 ENOCH 17. **20** 2 ENOCH 18. **21** 2 ENOCH 19. **22** 2 ENOCH 20-21. **23** 3 ENOCH 19–28.

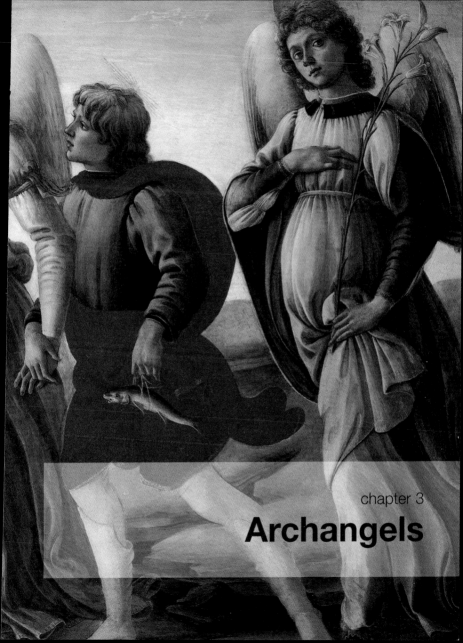

chapter 3
Archangels

Ruling Angels

The archangels are the first or ruling angels, but surprisingly, Dionysius ranks them eighth in the hierarchy. In the Bible they are what their name implies—ruling angels—although the name "archangel" is not in the Hebrew Scriptures. There are several traditions about them: a group of seven, or four, or three, and no general agreement about their names, apart from Michael, Gabriel, and Raphael.

Enoch saw seven groups of archangels in the sixth heaven.[1] Like all angels, these mighty beings were composite rather than single, and all were alike: equal height, brilliant faces, identical robes. They were seven and yet one. They controlled the creation, harmonizing everything in earth and heaven, controlling the movements of the stars, the seasons, the waters of the earth, and plant and animal life. They also kept a record of all human activity.

The Seven

St. John saw seven spirits before the heavenly throne. He called them the seven torches,[2] an ancient way of describing the unity and plurality of the angels. Seven individual flames can be distinguished, but burning together, they are seen as one. These seven torches were the menorah, the seven-branched temple lamp that gave one light, and in later tradition the seven lamps represented the Presence of the Lord on earth, the Light of the World. St. John saw the Lamb enthroned in

previous page: **Three Archangels and Tobias, Filippino Lippi, c.1480s, Italian**
The Book of Tobit mentions only Raphael as Tobias' guardian, but here Michael and Gabriel also travel with him.

right: **Archangel Michael, Baron Arlid Rosenkrantz, 1930s, Danish**

heaven with seven horns and seven eyes "which are the seven spirits of God."[3] The exalted human figure, "the Lamb," was all seven spirits, but was also One. His seven horns were beams of light—there is Hebrew symbolism underlying St. John's Greek text, in which beam and horn are the same word—and so the Lamb radiated the sevenfold divine Light of the World. Zechariah, the priest-prophet, about 500 B.C.E. described the seven lamps as the seven eyes of the Lord on earth, the seven archangels who were one Presence.[4]

St. John heard seven angels blow seven trumpets.[5] He saw seven identical angels coming from the holy of holies in white linen robes and golden girdles, the sanctuary dress of a high priest. They carried bowls of wrath. This was the sevenfold presence of the heavenly high priest, pouring divine judgement on the earth.[6] Levi, ancestor of the priestly tribe in Israel, had a vision of being vested in priestly garments by seven "men in white," seven angels. This empowered him to stand near the throne in heaven and to teach the heavenly mysteries on earth.[7] The Songs of the Sabbath Sacrifice show that the Dead Sea Scrolls community knew seven angel priests as the ruling princes of the heavenly sanctuary, and their War Scroll had seven vested high priests with trumpets leading the army on the Day of Vengeance.

The sevenfold Presence was an ancient temple tradition about the angels whose fire brought either illumination or judgment. Isaiah, a priest-prophet about 700 B.C.E., described the sevenfold Spirit resting on the Messiah and transforming his mind.[8] Ezekiel, a priest-prophet about 600 B.C.E., saw six angels bringing divine judgment on sinful Jerusalem, and a seventh, dressed as a scribe, marking the faithful so they would be spared.[9] In both cases, the seven were six-plus-one: the sevenfold Spirit was the Spirit of the Lord, plus six other "aspects" of the Spirit; and the six angels of judgment were distinguished from the one who marked the faithful. Six-plus-one was the pattern for the archangels. Philo, the first-century C.E. Jewish philosopher, said the menorah symbolized the One who both separated and joined together the six other powers. The archangels as six-plus-one also appear in early Christian texts; Hermas, a prophet in Rome about 100 C.E. had a vision of a tall man flanked by six others, three on each side, and was told they were the Son of God and six angels. An amethyst has been found, engraved: Raphael, Renel, Uriel, Ichthus, Michael, Gabriel, Azael, the six angels plus the Son in the center, since Ichthus, fish, was a common symbol for Jesus. When the seven-branched lamp was adapted for Christian use, the central stem became the cross, representing the Son, and the flanking angels who had been the six lamps on either side, became the six altar candles.

The names of the seven can vary. Enoch saw Uriel (or Suriel), Raphael, Raguel, Michael, Saraqael, Gabriel, and Remiel.[10] Michael, the most important, is in the center. Seven unnamed holy ones brought Enoch back to earth after his vision of the stars and the calendar,[11] and in another vision he saw seven white men: four who went to earth to bind the fallen angels, and three who took him up to see the vision. He also saw the seven "white ones" bringing out the rebel angels on the day of judgment.[12] In the *Merkavah Rabbah*, a Jewish mystical text where Enoch has been transformed into the great angel Metatron, the seven are named as Michael, Gabriel, Suriel, Aktariel, Rephael, Boriel, and Yomiel.

The Orthodox Church has another pattern: Michael plus seven other archangels: Gabriel, Raphael, Uriel, Selaphiel, Jehudiel, Barachiel, (Je)Remiel. There is a feast day in the East for all the angels on November 8, but churches are dedicated only to Michael and Gabriel. In response to growing concern, the Council of Laodicea in the fourth century forbade the worship or invocation of angels, and when a certain Aldebert caused a scandal in eighth-century Europe by invoking the seven archangels, Pope Zachary limited the named archangels to three: Michael, Gabriel, and Raphael. The Lateran Council in 745 C.E. approved a feast day for these three, but the other ancient names were forbidden. They were not forgotten. An obliterated fresco reappeared during the cleaning of a church in Palermo in 1516—the Almighty enthroned with seven archangels: Michael, "the victorious," Gabriel "the one who announces," Raphael "the healer," and then Uriel "the strong ally," Jehudiel "the one who brings recompense," Barachiel "the helper," and Sealtiel "the speaker." Churches dedicated to the seven began to be built, including the Basilica of St. Mary of the Angels in Rome, decorated by Michelangelo and consecrated in 1566.

right: **Adoration of the Lamb (detail), from the Beatus of Liébana, Silos Apocalypse, 1109, Spain**
Heaven and earth were one hierarchy. Here the Lamb is enthroned in heaven with the four living creatures and the fiery wheels before him. Below them are the saints and martyrs, with their halos and palms of victory, and below them, the ranks of the faithful on earth.

following page: **Seven Angels Pouring Vials of the Wrath of God upon the Earth, unknown painter, 19th century, British**
The seven archangels are the sevenfold presence of the Lord, symbolized by the seven lamps of the menorah. The plurality of the divine presence is the root of the Christian belief in the Trinity.

a genecu palmuf en dicena Benedicao aegiu a fupienaqu a graaqurum acaco a honor

funge filiorum erht sigmaa cen cu m quadragin au quacuor milu:

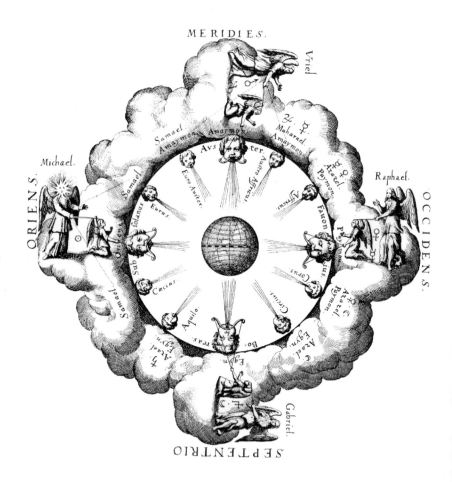

The Four and the Three

1 Enoch has the earliest description of four archangels: Michael, Uriel, Raphael, and Gabriel saw the destruction caused by the fallen angels, and took the prayers of their victims to the Most High. The four were sent down to imprison the fallen angels and restore the earth.[13] This story is repeated in Christian prophecies. The four names appear in an early Christian "letter" about the secret teaching of Jesus, and on an amulet found in a fifth century Christian tomb in Rome. These four took the bodies of Adam and Abel to Paradise.[14] In a vision of the holy of holies, Enoch saw the four "presences" or "faces" around the Lord: Michael, Gabriel, and Raphael, but the fourth was named Phanuel.[15] Among the Dead Sea Scrolls, the War Scroll used the names Michael, Gabriel, Raphael—and Sariel.[16] The leading archangel banned by Pope Zachary, then, was the archangel with many names: Uriel-Phanuel-Sariel meaning "the fire of God–the presence of God–the Prince of God."

In the Western Church, only three archangels were recognized by name: Michael, Gabriel, and Raphael. In Jewish tradition, these three appeared to Abraham at Mamre, to promise the birth of Isaac and to warn of the destruction of Sodom.[17]

left: **The Four Archangels and the Twelve Winds, Robert Fludd, 1626, British**

In the Psalms, angels are described with a Hebrew word that can mean wind or spirit, and in the Book of Revelation, St. John saw angels at the four corners of the earth, restraining the winds. Fludd believed that if there was one supreme God, he must have created both angels and demons, and so he said the winds were controlled by the archangels, but they delegated some of their power to the spirits of the air, the demons. Michael is shown here as the Prince of the sun.

Then the imperishable angels of immortal God
Michael, Gabriel, Raphael, and Uriel,
Who know what evils anyone did previously,
Lead all the souls of men from the murky dark
To judgment, to the tribunal of the great
Immortal God.

SIBYLLINE ORACLES 2.214–19

right: **The Three Archangels triumphing over Lucifer, Marco d'Oggiono, 1516, Italian**

In the Enoch tradition, the archangels Raphael, Gabriel, and Michael are sent to bring judgment on the fallen angels, whilst Uriel is sent to warn Noah of the impending flood. Here, Michael and two other archangels are putting the leader of the fallen angels into a pit in the desert. It is usually said that the Book of Enoch was lost to the Western Christian world until its rediscovery in Ethiopia in 1769. This picture suggests otherwise.

above: **The Hospitality of Abraham, mosaic, Church of San Vitale, Ravenna, 6th century, Italian**

Three angels ate and drank with Abraham at Mamre when they brought him news that Sarah was to have a son named Isaac. Elsewhere we are told that angels and spirits do not eat and drink, making this an unusual account.

above right: **Abraham and the Three Angels, Paolo Maurizio, late 16th century, Italian**

How shall we tell an angel
  From another guest?
How, from the common worldly herd,
  One of the blest?

GERTRUDE HALL, "ANGELS"

The Archangel Michael

The great and glorious angel is Michael, who has power over this people and governs them, he put the Law into the hearts of those who believe.

HERMAS PARABLE 8.3

Michael ("who is like God?") is the ruler of the archangels,[18] who prevented the fallen angels learning the Sacred Name that gave power over the creation. In the Hebrew Scriptures, the angel in charge of Israel is sometimes called Michael,[19] and sometimes the Lord.[20] He is the Great Prince, in charge of the seventh heaven,[21] often depicted holding a green palm branch in his left hand and a spear in his right, trampling the devil. He is the aspect of the Lord that appears as the mighty warrior defeating his enemies: "Who is like thee O Lord, among the gods?;" "Who among the sons of gods is like the Lord, a God feared in the council of the Holy Ones, greatly terrible above all around him?"[22] In the Book of Revelation, Michael and his angels fight "the ancient serpent, the Devil and Satan," but later in the book, the one who fights the Devil is called the Lord.[23]

right: **St. Michael Killing the Dragon, Josse Lieferinxe (Master of St. Sebastian), late 15th century, French**

Although it is a popular theme in art, there is no basis in Scripture or tradition for the story of Michael killing the dragon. In the Book of Revelation, Michael drives the dragon from heaven, but he survives to torment the earth. Later the dragon is bound in a pit for one thousand years, and then, after the great battle with the saints, is thrown into the lake of fire and sulphur.

Michael is a warrior priest, fighting evil and taking the prayers and souls of the righteous up to heaven. Michael drove Satan from heaven when he refused to worship Adam,[24] and he was sent to bind Semhaza the chief of the fallen angels.[25] Michael brought Solomon a magic ring to repel demons, so that they could not hinder the building of the temple.[26] The many St. Michael's Mounts show where he and his angels triumphed over ancient evils, and in the Western Church he became the patron of soldiers.

In later Jewish tradition, Michael was high priest at the altar in heaven. He had the keys to the Kingdom of heaven, and carried a huge bowl to take the prayers of the righteous to God. When he returned, he brought them the oil of life.[27] Adam had begged for this oil, but Michael said it was only for holy people in the last days.[28] Christian pilgrims to Jerusalem in the early centuries used to take home tiny flasks of "oil from the Tree of Life." The angel high priest burning incense in St. John's vision of heaven, could have been Michael or the Lord.[29]

Michael went to warn Abraham when he was near death, and then took him to heaven on a chariot of cherubim,[30] he disputed with Satan for the body of Moses, and he anointed Enoch and made him an angel.[31] Michael is mentioned in the Koran[32] and in Muslim tradition he has green and saffron wings, and ranks second after Gabriel.

left: **St. Michael weighing souls, stained glass window from St. Marys Church, Westwood, Bradford-on-Avon, Wiltshire, England**
St. Michael, here in the feathered angel costume used in medieval mystery plays, weighs the souls of the dead.

The Archangel Gabriel

Gabriel ("the mighty one of God") is Prince of the Host, in charge of the sixth heaven.[33] He is the aspect of the Lord that the Palmist described as his strength: "Thou who art enthroned upon the cherubim, shine forth … arouse thy strength and come to save us."[34] St. Paul wrote: "…lead a life worthy of the Lord … strengthened with all power according to his glorious might."[35]

Gabriel appeared to Daniel to interpret visions and prophecies about the future Messiah,[36] and to Zechariah and to Mary to announce the birth of John the Baptist and Jesus, the Messiah.[37] Second in rank after Michael, in early pictures he carries a sword, but later a lily. Gabriel was sent to destroy the demon children of the fallen angels [38] and was in charge of Paradise, the cherubim, and the powers.[39] In icons, Gabriel can be depicted with a branch from Paradise, carrying a lantern or a mirror. In 1951 the Pope declared him the patron of telecommunication workers.

Some of the first Christians thought of Gabriel as the Holy Spirit and the inspiration of Scripture. The Angel of the Holy Spirit, they said, inspired the Psalms and spoke through the faithful, and together with the Lord was worshiped in heaven. The early Christian prophet "Isaiah" had his own vision of the heavenly throne, but instead of two seraphim,[40] he saw the Lord on the right of the throne and the angel of the Holy Spirit on the left.[41] Origen's Jewish teacher had the same idea: Isaiah's two seraphim were the Son of God and the Holy Spirit,[42] and in one account of the resurrection, Michael and the angel of the Holy Spirit carry Jesus from the tomb on their shoulders, like the seraphim supporting the heavenly throne.[43] Since Michael stands on the right hand and Gabriel on the left in Jewish tradition, this is another sign that Michael and the Lord could have been identical figures,

above: **Archangel Gabriel, on a column in the church of Nôtre-Dame, Chauvigny, 12th century, French**

An angel of the Lord appeared to shepherds in Bethlehem to announce the birth of the Messiah, and a host of angels sang "Glory to God in the Highest and on earth peace, goodwill toward men." The angel was probably Gabriel, as he appears elsewhere as the messenger in the Nativity story.

as were Gabriel and the Holy Spirit. On the other hand Christ, Michael, and Gabriel is a possible meaning of the XMΓ symbol used in Syria, and in one account of the Annunciation, the Lord took the form of Gabriel as he became incarnate in Mary.[44]

Gabriel (Jibril) is mentioned twice in the Koran.[45] Gabriel revealed the Koran to Muhammad, and scholars think Gabriel is the Spirit of Faith and Truth,[46] the honorable Messenger from before the throne[47] and the Holy Spirit.[48] In Muslim tradition, Gabriel was one of the three angels who came to Abraham, and he gave Solomon his magic ring.

right: **The Archangel Gabriel, from *The Wonders of Creation and the Oddities of Existence*, c.1375–1425, Islamic**
In the Koran, Gabriel is never described as an angel, as though to distinguish him from the other ranks. He is the one who brings down the word of God.

following page: **The Annunciation, Fra Angelico, 1430s, Italian**
Although this seems to be Mary at home looking out onto her garden, the curious lighting shows that we are in fact in the temple. The even light around Mary indicates the holy of holies, which was all light, and the garden is the great hall of the temple which represented Eden. Gabriel, the fiery archangel, is permitted to enter the holy of holies because of his high rank, to tell the Queen about her Son.

وَمِنْهُمْ جِبْرَئِيلُ

Trinitatis nobile Triclinium

In the sixth month the angel Gabriel was sent from God to a city of Galilee named Nazareth, to a virgin betrothed to a man whose name was Joseph, of the house of David; and the virgin's name was Mary. And he came to her and said, "Hail, O favored One, the Lord is with you. Blessed are you among women." But she was greatly troubled at his saying, and considered in her mind what sort of greeting this might be. And the angel said to her, "Do not be afraid Mary, for you have found favor with God. And behold, you will conceive in your womb and bear a son, and you shall call his name Jesus."

LUKE 1

left: **The Annunciation, Arthur Hughes, 19th century, British**
Gabriel is often shown holding a lily, but here the archangel hovers over them.
Mary is spinning red wool, a motif drawn from icons of the Annunciation,
and the Holy Spirit, in the form of a dove, prepares to come upon her.

The Archangel Raphael

Raphael ("healing of God") was set over the demons, and healed the damage they had done.[49] He is the healing aspect of the Lord: "Return O faithless sons, I will heal your faithlessness."[50] Similairly Jesus said: "I will come and heal him."[51]

The Great Holy One commanded Raphael to bind and imprison Azazel, and heal the earth of the plagues the fallen angels had brought with their abuse of knowledge.[52] He was one of Enoch's guides in heaven and taught him about the Tree of Wisdom.[53] He was set over the spirits of human beings, and watched over them even after death as they waited for the Day of Judgment.[54]

Raphael appears in the Book of Tobit, as the guardian and guide of his son Tobias. The story, set in Mesopotamia, shows how the prayers of Jewish families were answered. God sent Raphael to heal Tobit, who had lost his sight, and to rescue Sarah from a demon named Asmodeus, who had killed all her suitors. To accompany him on his journey to Sarah, Tobias hired a man servant, not knowing he was Raphael in human form. When they camped for the night, Tobias caught a fish, and Raphael told him to keep the heart and liver to drive away demons, and the gall as a cure for blindness. At their destination, Tobias burned the heart and liver, and the stench drove

right: The Archangel Raphael warns Adam and Eve, illustration to *Paradise Lost*, William Blake, 1808, British
In John Milton's *Paradise Lost*, Book 5, the Archangel Raphael was sent to warn Adam and Eve of Satan's plan to cause their downfall. They sat on grassy seats to have lunch together in the Garden, and then Raphael warned them that they would be happy like the angels only as long as they were obedient like the angels.

away Asmodeus so that he could safely marry Sarah. They returned home to his blind father and restored his sight with the fish gall. Then the angel revealed who he was.

Raphael told them all about angels. He was one of the seven who presented prayers to the Holy One in heaven, and he had carried their prayers to God. God had commanded him to help them—so the angel did not act of his own free will. He had been only a vision for them, proved by the fact that they had not seen him eat or drink. (Compare here Jesus's words on Easter day, when he appeared to the disciples in Jerusalem, and had to convince them he was not just a spirit or a vision: " 'Have you anything here to eat?' They gave him a piece of broiled fish and he took it and ate before them."[55])

Raphael, sometimes the patron of travelers, is depicted carrying the fish, or holding a jar of medication while Tobias carries the fish.

left: **Tobias Returns Sight to his Father, Rembrandt, 1636, Dutch**
In the Book of Tobit, the Archangel Raphael told Tobias to anoint the eyes of his blind father with fish gall so that he would be able to see again. This is a story with two meanings: angels also give vision in the sense that they enable spiritual sight.

The Archangel Uriel

Uriel! for thou of those sev'n Spirits that stand
In sight of God's high throne, gloriously bright,
The first art wont his great authentic will
Interpreter through highest Heaven to bring,
Where all his Sons thy Embassy attend;
And here art likeliest by supreme decree
Like honour to obtain, and as his eye
To visit oft this new Creation round...

JOHN MILTON, *PARADISE LOST*, BOOK 3

Uriel ("fire of God") or Oriel ("light of God"), was also known as Phanuel ("the Presence of God"), and Sariel ("the Presence of God"). He is the aspect of the Lord as fire: "The light of Israel will be a fire and his Holy One a flame."[56] Jesus also said: "I came to cast fire on the earth."[57] Uriel was sent to warn Noah of the flood,[58] and in later Jewish tradition he was the cherub with the fiery sword who barred the gate to Eden. He was set over the whole world and over the underworld,[59] and was understandably described as "the strong ally." He wrestled with Jacob after he had met a hostile army of angels,[60] and Jacob named the

right: **Fiery cherub guarding the gates, The Expulsion from Paradise, mosaic, Monreale Cathedral, 13th century, Italian**
The Lord, here as an angel, made garments of skin for Adam and Eve and then drove them from Eden. The Bible says cherubim barred their way to the tree of life, but here it is a six-winged fiery seraph, whom later tradition said was Uriel.

HIC·EXPVLIT ADĀ·7·EVĀ·DE
PISO·DS·7·POSVIT·CHERVBIN
TODE·CV·FLAMEO·GLADIO

Jacob was left alone; and a man wrestled with him until the breaking of the day. When the man saw that he did not prevail against Jacob, he touched the hollow of his thigh; and Jacob's thigh was put out of joint as he wrestled with him. Then he said "Let me go, for the day is breaking." But Jacob said, "I will not let you go unless you bless me." And he said to him "What is your name?" And he said, "Jacob." Then he said, "Your name shall no more be called Jacob but Israel, for you have striven with God and with men and have prevailed." Then Jacob asked him, "Tell me, I pray, your name." But he said, "Why is it that you ask my name?" And there he blessed him. So Jacob called the name of the place Peniel, saying, "For I have seen God face to face and yet my life is preserved."

GENESIS 32.24-30

right: **Jacob wrestling with the Angel, Louis Leloir, 19th century, French**
On the night Jacob returned home and was preparing to meet his brother Esau, he encountered an angel who wrestled with him until dawn. Tradition says the Angel was Uriel, and that he changed Jacob's name to Israel meaning "the one who strives with God." Another meaning for Israel is "the man who has seen God."

place Peniel, "Face of God," similar to Phanuel, another name for Uriel. Uriel helped Solomon repel demons from the temple.[61] He guarded the fallen angels in prison, and on the day of judgment would bring out all who had been false gods.[62] He was banned by Pope Zachary after a scandal involving the invocation of the archangels, and so pictures of him are rare. He is depicted with a fiery sword, or with a flame in his hand.

Uriel, Michael, and Raphael were all Enoch's guides on his heavenly journey, and Uriel answered his questions about the pattern of the stars and rebel stars who were the fallen angels. He then revealed to Enoch all the secrets of the calendar, because he was the archangel who guided the stars.[63] The ancient astronomy book in 1 Enoch is a remarkable and detailed scientific text, the only known example of angel teaching, and it is attributed to Uriel, the angel who illumined the mind. By keeping Adam and Eve from Eden, he barred them from the ancient knowledge that Eden symbolized.

Uriel was an important angel after the temple was destroyed in 70 C.E., revealing to Ezra the meaning of his visions and helping him understand the disaster.[64] He may also have been the Prince of Light mentioned in the Dead Sea Scrolls. In Egyptian Gnosticism, he was the second of the four great light givers, the power who perceived truth, enabling both reception and memory, and Gabriel was his attendant.[65]

left: **Archangel Uriel, window in Holy Trinity Church, Tansley, Derbyshire, Ford Maddox Brown, 19th century, British**
Uriel, who revealed the secrets of the calendar to Enoch, is vested because he is an archangel. His cape is embroidered with astronomical signs, and also shows Adam and Eve whom he barred from Eden. His halo is the face of the sun, and he holds a book because he illuminates the mind.

Interview with The Rt. Rev. Dr. Geoffrey Rowell

Anglican Bishop of Gibraltar in Europe

What is the role of angels in the life of an Anglican Christian?

In common with all Christians who use formal liturgies, every time Anglicans celebrate the Eucharist they are reminded in the words of the Eucharistic prayer that their prayer and praise are joined "with angels and archangels and with all the company of heaven," as they echo the words of the Sanctus, the angelic song of heaven. At Christmas, popular hymns and carols take up the theme of the angelic annunciation of the incarnation to Mary, and the praise of the angels rejoicing in the birth of Christ. "Hark the herald angels sing!" and "It came upon the midnight clear" are two obvious examples. Christian poets such as George Herbert and Thomas Traherne in the seventeenth century have a lively sense of the power and protection of angels, and in more recent times angels feature in both the Christian apologetic and imaginative writing of C. S. Lewis.

In England and Wales there are 324 churches dedicated to St. Michael and All Angels, and the feast of Michaelmas is a major festival both in the Book of Common Prayer and in more recent liturgical revision. In the prayers at Compline, or Night Prayer, as the blessing of God is invoked upon the place where the office has been prayed, the presence of God's holy angels is asked that "we may be preserved in peace." Similar prayers would be used at the blessing of houses or the dedication of churches.

In countless stained glass windows in traditional parish churches, angels, and especially St. Michael the archangel, are depicted as guardians and protectors, and they are also depicted on many war memorials and in dramatic sculptures such as that of St. Michael at Coventry Cathedral.

Sorrowing or guardian angels are characteristic of many nineteenth century memorials in cemeteries and churchyards. There are also splendid examples of painted or carved church roofs and vaults, in which angels remind congregations of the worship of heaven. Imaginative depictions of angels are often characteristic themes of modern church art and textiles.

Despite the influence of "demythologizing" in some academic theology, which would dismiss angels as the symbolic language of a past age, more recent times have seen a renewed sense of angels as agents of God's grace and goodness, and as protecting powers against the forces of evil. In the wider Anglican Communion, many Anglican churches in the developing world, especially in Africa, have a lively awareness of angels as guides, guardians, and protectors.

NOTES

1 2 ENOCH 19. **2** REVELATION 4. **3** REVELATION 5. **4** ZECHARIAH 4. **5** REVELATION 8-9. **6** REVELATION 15. **7** THE TESTAMENT OF LEVI 2 & 8. **8** ISAIAH 11. **9** EZEKIEL 9. **10** 1 ENOCH 20. **11** 1 ENOCH 81. **12** 1 ENOCH 90. **13** 1 ENOCH 9-10. **14** APOCALYPSE OF MOSES 40. **15** 1 ENOCH 40. **16** WAR SCROLL IX. **17** GENESIS 18. **18** 1 ENOCH 24. **19** DANIEL 12. **20** DEUTERONOMY 32.8-9. **21** 3 ENOCH 17. **22** EXODUS 15.11 AND PSALM 89.6-7. **23** REVELATION 12 AND 19-20. **24** LIFE OF ADAM AND EVE 14. **25** 1 ENOCH 10. **26** TESTAMENT OF SOLOMON. **27** 3 BARUCH 11& 15. **28** APOCALYPSE OF MOSES 13. **29** REVELATION 8. **30** TESTAMENT OF ABRAHAM. **31** 2 ENOCH 22. **32** SURA 2.92. **33** 3 ENOCH 17. **34** PSALM 80.2-3 **35** COLOSSIANS 1.10-11 **36** DANIEL 8 & 9. **37** LUKE 1. **38** 1 ENOCH 10. **39** 1 ENOCH 20 & 54. **40** ISAIAH 6. **41** ASCENSION OF ISAIAH 4, 9, 11. **42** FIRST PRINCIPLES 1.3. **43** ASCENSION OF ISAIAH 3. **44** EPISTLE OF THE APOSTLES. **45** SURAS 2.97–8 & 66.4. **46** SURA 26.193. **47** SURA 81.19-21. **48** SURA 2.87, 253. **49** 1 ENOCH 40. **50** JEREMIAH 3.22. **51** MATTHEW 8.7. **52** 1 ENOCH 10. **53** 1 ENOCH 32. **54** 1 ENOCH 22. **55** LUKE 24. **56** ISAIAH 10. **57** LUKE 12.49 **58** 1 ENOCH 10. **59** 1 ENOCH 20. **60** GENESIS 32. **61** TESTAMENT OF SOLOMON 2. **62** 1 ENOCH 19, 21, 27. **63** 1 ENOCH 72. **64** 2 ESDRAS 4,5 & 20. **65** GOSPEL OF THE EGYPTIANS.

chapter 4

The Chariot Throne

The Seraphim

In the year that King Uzziah died, I saw the Lord, sitting upon a throne, high and lifted up, and his train filled the temple. Above him stood the seraphim; each had six wings: with two he covered his face, and with two he covered his feet, and with two he flew.

ISAIAH 6

In the height of heaven and in the midst of the angel hosts was the throne of God, glimpsed by the prophets Isaiah, Ezekiel, Daniel, and St. John. Each tried to describe what he had seen: Isaiah and Daniel left only very brief accounts, but Ezekiel and St. John attempted more detail. They were clearly stretching words to their limit, trying to convey something of the Glory they had seen.

Isaiah's vision is the earliest biblical description of the angels as winged beings. He saw the Lord in the holy of holies, enthroned

previous page: **Ascension of Christ (detail), Rabula Gospels, 6th century, Syrian**

This is a rare example of early Christian art, and shows the Ascension of Jesus but not as described by St. Luke. The artist imagined Jesus going to heaven in the fiery chariot throne described by Ezekiel, who saw cherubim, wheels within wheels, and a sapphire throne where the human form of the Lord was enthroned in glory. Here Jesus is depicted as that human form. The fiery cherub has four heads and wings full of eyes, and beneath the wings, as in Ezekiel's vision, there is a human hand. There is a wheel within a wheel, and attendant angels veil their hands to offer holy things—the crowns of victory for the Lord who has conquered death.

beneath the seraphim.[1] We do not know how many there were; sometimes an artist depicts two, with the Lord enthroned between them, but a later tradition said there were four, corresponding to the four winds at the four corners of the world.[2] This is why four great seraphim are often depicted in churches at the four corners supporting the dome of heaven.

Each seraph had six wings: with two he covered his face, with two he covered his feet, and with two he flew. Usually thought to mean that each covered himself with his wings, a Seraph can be depicted as just a cluster of six wings, but some early Christians thought the wings were covering the Lord on the throne. Origen[3] said that the wings covered the face and feet of the One on the throne, thus veiling him, and showing that it was impossible to know everything about the Lord.[4] He also said that the two seraphim were the Son of God and the Holy Spirit.

The name seraph suggests a burning one, the Hebrew *saraph* meaning to burn. Since all the angels were fiery, there must have been something special about the fire of the seraphim. As the highest rank, they stood closest to the throne and were the first to transmit the light, warmth, and purity of God to the lower ranks. Isaiah was purified by a seraph and made a messenger from the Lord, meaning that the fire had transformed him into an angel; and Enoch was transformed into fire when he became the ruling angel Metatron.[5] Thus the seraphim burned away the material bodies of those who were becoming angels. Later Jewish tradition, however, said they burned up the accusations that Satan brought against Israel.[6]

Let the bright seraphim in burning row,
Their loud, uplifted angel trumpets blow.
Let the cherubic host, in tuneful choirs,
Touch their immortal harps with golden wires.

NEWBURGH HAMILTON, "ORATORIO SAMSON"

left: **The Last Judgment (detail, Fiery Seraphim), fresco in the Church of Santa Cecilia in Trastevere, Rome, Pietro Cavallini, 1293, Italian**
The fiery seraphim flank the throne, above the blue-winged cherubim and the rest of the angel host.

The Cherubim

Ezekiel's visions of the throne are the greatest and most mysterious of all such visions in the Bible, and he described the cherubim. He saw the Glory of the Lord leaving the polluted temple in Jerusalem and appearing among the exiles in Babylon. The language used is so strange that we cannot be certain of the details, but he seems to describe a fiery chariot with four living creatures, beneath the Glory of the Lord on his throne.[7] Such a description is unique in the Bible, but Ezekiel was a priest in the Jerusalem temple about 600 B.C.E., and these must be angels as he knew them. This description of the chariot throne was thought to be so disturbing that it was forbidden for anyone but a scholar to read it.[8]

The Hebrew of "the chapter of the chariot" is very obscure, mixing masculine and feminine forms, singular and plural. Perhaps Ezekiel was trying to describe the unity and plurality of the divine presence. The four living creatures—elsewhere he calls them the cherubim—seem to have been fiery female humanoids, with bovine feet and four wings—two outstretched and two covering her body. Each had four faces—a man, a lion, an ox, and an eagle—and in the midst of them was a great fire. They moved together like a flash of lightning, and around them was a wheel within a wheel—the first time we hear of these mysterious "wheels." Something in the vision—possibly the wheels—was full of eyes or points of light, and above them was a firmament like sapphire. There the prophet saw the Lord in human form, enthroned and wreathed in a rainbow.[9] Ezekiel received a scroll from the One on the throne, meaning that he was given special knowledge to be a prophet.[10]

There is a second description of the chariot, this time leaving the temple,[11] where the living creatures are described as cherubim with wheels, and there was something whirling beneath them. One of the faces was different too, a cherub instead of an ox. A man clothed in linen took fiery coals from the whirling place and scattered them on Jerusalem to destroy it. Then Ezekiel saw the cherubim and the wheels take up the Glory of the Lord and carry it away.[12]

Ezekiel left another description of a cherub, this time in the Garden of Eden.[13] Even though the cherub is compared to the King of Tyre (an enemy of Jerusalem), there is no doubt that she is a female figure, the anointed guardian angel who had walked amidst the sons of fire— the fiery creatures Ezekiel described in his chariot vision. She was full of wisdom and perfect in beauty, and vested with the jewels of a high priest! When she became a proud cherub and corrupted her heavenly wisdom, she was cast out and burned to ashes on the earth.

Moses placed two of these winged humanoid cherubim on the mercy seat over the ark in the holy of holies. They were made of gold, and set face to face with wings outstretched. When the Lord came to the tabernacle, he appeared between them.[14] In Solomon's temple, two huge golden cherubim formed the chariot throne in the holy of holies,[15] and so the psalmists sang of the Lord enthroned on the Cherubim.[16] They also sang of the Lord flying on a cherub—presumably this chariot—when he came to help his servants in distress.[17]

Two-headed cherubim—a human head and a lion head— were depicted between palm trees on the walls and doors of the temple,[18] and embroidered on the veil that screened the holy of holies.[19] Most familiar of all, perhaps, are the cherubim and the whirling sword of fire which were set at the entrance to Eden to prevent Adam and Eve returning to the Garden, and blocking their way to the Tree of Life.[20]

previous page left: **The Vision of Ezekiel, Bear Bible, 17th century, Swiss**
In the Hebrew Scriptures, the most vivid description of the angels of the chariot
throne is found in Ezekiel. Here, the fiery storm cloud appears to him as he
stands by the river Chebar in Babylon. He saw four living creatures, each with
four faces and four wings, and the wheels within wheels. In the midst of the
living creatures was a moving fire. Above them all was enthroned "the likeness
of the Glory of the Lord."

previous page right: **The Vision of Ezekiel, Raphael, 1518, Italian**
Ezekiel saw a storm cloud, encircling the likeness of the Glory of the Lord
enthroned above the four living creatures. Raphael does not depict what Ezekiel
described—the winged tetramorphs with bovine feet. He has taken the four
living creatures from St. John's vision—the lion, the ox, the man, and the eagle—
but has not given them the six wings full of eyes. There is no throne above a
sapphire pavement and no encircling rainbow. This is an imaginative piece,
rather than an illustration of Ezekiel's text.

left: **Cherubim on the Ark of the Covenant, c. 1280, French**
The ark of the covenant was kept in the holy of holies, and above it was the
mercy seat, flanked by two cherubim. Here, the Lord appeared to Moses and to
Aaron. In the temple this became the great cherub throne, where the Lord
appeared to Isaiah. Philo, the Jewish philosopher who lived in the time of Jesus,
said the two cherubim on the ark symbolized the two greatest heavenly powers:
the creative power, called God, and the kingly power, called the Lord, and the
divine presence was discerned between them. Their outstretched wings showed
that the whole world was protected by these powers. He explained that the
name cherubim meant "recognition and full knowledge," but nobody knows how
he came to this conclusion. Christian tradition built on Philo and taught that the
cherubim are those who know God, who are filled with Wisdom and then pour
this onto others.

The Lord God drove out the man; and at the east of the garden of Eden he placed the cherubim, and a flaming sword which turned every way, to guard the way to the tree of life.

GENESIS 3

right: **Adam and Eve expelled from Paradise, Juan Correa,
17th century, Mexican**
The cherubim are the highest rank of angels of knowledge, and so it was a cherub who barred Adam and Eve from the Tree of Life, the source of Wisdom. Once they had chosen secular knowledge, Adam and Eve no longer had access to the life-giving knowledge of the angels.

Iudicium sedis
Ali[?]rupeum
sua

The Wheels

In a dream vision, Daniel saw the throne established over a great sea.[23] He described no seraphim, cherubim or living creatures, only the heavenly host and the fiery wheels of the throne (Ophannim), later identified as angels. Four terrible beasts had emerged from the sea, one after another, and during the time of the fourth beast, the great throne was set up. It was made of fire, had wheels of fire, and from it flowed streams of fire. On it sat the Ancient of Days, and before Him was the host of holy ones, ten thousand times ten thousand. When the books were opened for the day of judgment, a human figure rose up to heaven on clouds, and was enthroned. Jesus identified himself as this figure,[24] and so this throne vision became an important prophecy for Christians.

left: Daniel's vision of the four beasts from the sea, from the Beatus of Liébana (Silos Apocalypse), 1109, Spanish

Daniel saw the chariot throne in a night vision. First he saw four beasts: a lion with eagle's wings, a bear, a leopard with four heads and four wings, and a dreadful beast with iron teeth. Then he saw the Ancient of Days, with white robes and white hair, sat on the fiery throne with wheels of fire. A stream of fire flowed from it, and a vast host of angels stood around as the books were opened for the Judgment. A human figure—"one like a son of man"—was given dominion and power over the earth, and this must be the figure depicted here. He has a cross in his halo—a sign that he is Christ—and he is not wearing the white robes of the Ancient of Days.

Round the throne were twenty four thrones, and seated on the thrones were twenty four elders, clad in white garments, with golden crowns upon their heads. From the throne issued flashes of lightning, and voices and peals of thunder, and before the throne burn seven torches of fire, which are the seven spirits of God.

REVELATION 4.4-5

right: **The Throne in Heaven, digital illustration, David Miles, 2003, British**
St. John saw the throne, set in the midst of the highest ranks of angels. There were four living creatures "full of eyes in front and behind," and the seven torches of fire, here the menorah, representing the seven archangels who were the presence of God. In the outer circle were the angel priests—twenty four elders wearing white robes and golden crowns, and offering incense. They worshiped the One on the throne, praising him as the Source of all creation.

Christian Tradition

St. John's is the only vision of the throne in the New Testament.[25] Like Ezekiel, he saw four living creatures, each with a different face—a lion, an ox, an eagle, and a man—and with six wings full of eyes. Around the throne he saw twenty-four elders in white robes wearing golden crowns, also seated on thrones. Before the throne were seven fiery spirits, and beyond them, the host of angels were worshiping the Lamb.

The living creatures as described by John became symbols of the evangelists: Matthew (the man), Mark (the lion), Luke (the ox), and John (the eagle). Irenaeus, a bishop in France who died about 200 C.E., said the living creatures announced the presence of the Lord in the Hebrew Scriptures, just as the gospels did in the New Testament, and so there had to be four gospels.[26] Jesus often appears with the living creatures as the Lord enthroned, and this is sometimes explained as Jesus with the four evangelists.

The angels in the four throne visions in the Bible—the seraphim, the cherubim, and the wheels—thus correspond to the highest ranks of angels described in Dionysius' *Celestial Hierarchy*. Daniel's wheels are usually identified as Dionysius' thrones, since the throne was a wheeled chariot. It became the custom to depict Isaiah's seraphim in red robes, Ezekiel's living creatures/cherubim in blue robes, and the thrones in gold.

right: **The Vision of St. John (detail), from the Altarpiece of St. John the Baptist and St. John the Evangelist, Hans Memling, 1474–79, Flemish**
Memling correctly depicted the heavenly throne as the altar in a church, and an angel vested as a deacon explains the vision to St. John. In the Orthodox Christian tradition, the altar is known as the throne, a living reminder of the chariot throne and the angels who served it.

Chariot Throne Mystics

The chariot throne and the angels inspired the Jewish mystical writings known as the Hekhalot texts, and the mystics who wrote them were called Merkavah (chariot) mystics. Nobody knows the age of these writings, and the images in the texts are drawn from temple worship and the holy of holies. They list the ranks and names of the angels, and describe the guardians of the seven heavenly temples and the captains of the heavenly hosts. They depict angels bathing in rivers of fire and putting on their robes of hashmal. Nobody knows what that word means, or what the angels wore. Sometimes it is translated "color of amber," sometimes "gleaming bronze." Ezekiel saw hashmal in the midst of the fiery cloud that carried the throne, and hashmal surrounding the Glory of the Lord.

Several texts describe how a person can prepare with prayer and purification and then ascend to stand before the throne. There, he learns the secrets at the heart of creation: how the chariot "works" (Ma'aseh Merkavah), or how the creation "works" (Ma'aseh Bereshit). The journey is hindered by hostile angels who guard the doors to the innermost palace of the King, but eventually the worthy mystic reaches his goal and then returns to teach his disciples.

There is no single picture of heaven and the ascent because the texts were written in various times and places, but we can see in them the angel world of the Book of Revelation. The Jewish mystic passes within the circle of the living creatures and approaches the throne itself, set high above the other angels, just like the Lamb in St. John's vision. Other Jewish texts also knew that pious people could be ranked above the angels because the original Adam had been created greater than the angels.[27]

Jesus was the greatest Merkavah mystic. At his baptism he saw the heavens open and heard he was the Son of God. In the desert he was with the living creatures (usually thought of as ordinary desert animals), and the angels served him. This was the ascent experience described in Revelation 5, where the Lamb passes through the ranks of heaven to ascend the divine throne. He receives and opens the scroll—the knowledge—because he is worthy, and becomes one with the supreme power in heaven. Jesus had to overcome the lower angels hostile to his ascent, the principalities and powers.[28] He had risen above "all rule and authority and power and dominion, and above every name that is named not only in this age but in the age to come,"[29] and, bearing the Sacred Name, had been enthroned above all ranks of angels.[30]

The golden chariot of the cherubim that spread their wings and covered the ark of the covenant of the Lord.

1 CHRONICLES 28

above: **Christ in the Desert (detail), James J. Tissot, 1886–94, French**

After his baptism, when he had seen the heavens open, and heard the voice
declaring that he was the divine Son, Jesus went into the desert to wrestle with
the implication of the revelation. The devil tempted him to take an easier path, but
Jesus resisted. When the conflict was over, angels came and ministered to him,
says Matthew.

Metatron

The most important angel in the *Merkavah* texts is Metatron, whose name probably means "throne sharer." He is described in 3 Enoch as the greatest of the archangels, enthroned by the Holy One at the entrance to the highest heaven, and and then given the titles "lesser Yahweh" and "my servant." He had a glorious robe and a crown bearing the Sacred Name, the letters that created the world. The mysteries of the creation were revealed to him, and all the heavenly powers fell down before him. Metatron was the heavenly high priest, the angel who came with the Name of Yahweeh.

Rabbi Elisha ben Abuya was a Jewish mystic in the early second century C.E. When he had a vision and saw Metatron enthroned, he said there must be two powers in heaven. This was like the contemporary Christian teaching that Jesus was enthroned in heaven, but for a Jew this was heresy. 3 Enoch says a heavenly voice called for the apostates to return to the truth, all except Elisha ben Abuya for whom there was no hope. The voice ordered Metatron to leave his throne and be punished with sixty fiery lashes, so that nobody would ever again think there was a second power in heaven.

Rabbi Ishmael, a contemporary of R. Elisha, had a vision of heaven that is described in 3 Enoch. He learned that Enoch had been transformed into Metatron. The mysterious story in Genesis 5 says only that Enoch walked among the 'elohim and God took him, but 3 Enoch shows what happened to him. Metatron must have been an important angel for the first Christians, because in Philippians 2 Jesus is described as Metatron, the Servant who was exalted, given the Sacred Name, and then worshiped by all creation.

Interview with Rabbi Geoffrey W. Dennis

Rabbi of Congregation Kol Ami in Flower Mound, Texas, USA

What is the role of Angels in Jewish Tradition and Folklore?

From ancient times, Jewish tradition has recognized that God's manifold creation includes spiritual as well as material entities. In the Bible, there are a wondrous variety of numinous creatures that serve the God of Israel: Seraphim (Fiery Ones), Cherubim (Mighty Ones), Chayyot ([Holy] Beasts), Sarim (Princes), Ophanim (Wheels), and Melachim (Messengers). These creatures, collectively known as B'nei ha-Elohim (Divine Beings) and/or Kedoshim (holy ones), are assembled into an Adat El (divine assembly). Most of these entities are anonymous, but a few (three to be precise) have names: Michael, Gabriel, and Satan.

Subsequently all these divine beings are subsumed under the term malach (messenger/angel). The nature of these beings is subject to diverse, sometimes wildly different, interpretation. Some Jews have seen them as embodied divine will, others regarded them as purely spiritual personalities. Still other Jews understood them as synonymous with natural causality.

Driven by the demands of pure monotheism, Judaism likewise counts (though uncomfortably so) demons among God's agents. Thus it is accepted that various demonic entities, satanim (adversaries), melachei mashchit (destructive angels), shedim (evil spirits), and even the dreaded Malach ha-Mavet, the Angel of Death, have a role in the inscrutable workings of the divine plan.

Jewish myths and folklore tend to radically personify and personalize this angelic world: Angels are accorded spheres of influence. Names of angels are known and invoked for the benefit of mortals. Angels serve not only as messengers of God but as guardians of Israel. And angels are subject to emotions, such as envy and lust. These elements provide the impetus to a mythic world view that has yielded a vast and varied Jewish literature of angel and demon narratives.

Some of the more notable features of Jewish angelology include: a belief that a sort of rivalry exists between angels and humanity, but that man (being made in God's image) has the advantage, with the potential power to summon and command angels and demons. Also, Jewish angelology holds that the divide between the human and angelic is permeable; exemplary humans, such as Enoch, Elijah, and Sareh bat Asher, have achieved angelic status.

Drawing on this notion of affinity between angels and mortals, over the past millennium Jews have increasingly internalized and psychologized the meaning of angels; they have come to be understood, as in Hasidism, as by-products of human moral action, or, as in Liberal Judaism, as personifications of human motivations.

NOTES

1 ISAIAH 6. **2** REVELATION 7 AND 3 ENOCH 26. **3** DIED 253CE. **4** ON FIRST PRINCIPLES 4.3.
5 3 ENOCH 15. **6** 3 ENOCH 26. **7** EZEKIEL 1. **8** MISHNAH MEGILLAH 4. **9** EZEKIEL 1. **10** EZEKIEL
3. **11** EZEKIEL 10. **12** EZEKIEL 11. **13** EZEKIEL 28. **14** EXODUS 25.22 AND LEVITICUS 16.2.
15 1 CHRONICLES 28. **16** PSALM 80 AND PSALM 99. **17** PSALM 18 = 2 SAMUEL 22. **18** 1 KINGS 6
AND EZEKIEL 41. **19** 2 CHRONICLES 3. **20** GENESIS 3. **21** QUESTIONS ON EXODUS 2.62-65.
22 LIFE OF MOSES 2.97. **23** DANIEL 7. **24** MARK 14.62. **25** REVELATION 4. **26** AGAINST HERESIES
3.11.11 **27** GENESIS RABBAH 21. **28** COLOSSIANS 2 **29** EPHESIANS 1.21 **30** HEBREWS 1.

chapter 5

Angels in Worship

The Thrice Holy Hymn

Isaiah had the earliest known vision of angels when he was in the Jerusalem temple in 742 B.C.E.[1] He saw six-winged seraphim worshiping the Lord on his heavenly throne, and he heard them calling to each other with voices that shook the whole building:

Holy, Holy, Holy is the Lord of Hosts.

The whole earth is full of his glory.

These words, known as the "Thrice Holy Hymn," have been included in worship ever since. Whenever they are used, they remind even the smallest group of worshipers that they are close to the angels, worshiping with the host of heaven.

Isaiah was in the temple, mystically looking beyond the veil and into the holy of holies itself. He was gazing into the heart of the creation, where he saw fiery seraphim praising the Creator. From their place by the throne the seraphim looked out onto the whole world and saw that it was full of the glory of the Lord. Thus Isaiah believed that angelic praise of the Lord was at the heart of the creation, and the glory of the world around him flowed from this heavenly praise.

One of the seraphim then touched Isaiah's mouth with a glowing coal from the altar, and he was appointed the messenger or angel of the Lord of Hosts. Isaiah not only saw the heavenly worship; he was himself a part of it, and when he had been touched by the fire, he too became the angel of the Lord. He must have spoken about his vision, and so we know that the angels and their praises in heaven were a part of temple worship in Jerusalem in the eighth century B.C.E.

previous page: **Angel Relief, Pierre-Jean David D'Angers, 19th century, French**

Angels around the throne worshiping God is the best known image of heaven.

The harmony in heaven, shown by the praise and worship of the angels, had to be copied by the rest of the creation if there was to be peace and harmony on earth. The angels at Bethlehem, described by Luke in his nativity story, were singing about this: "Glory to God in the highest"—this was the worship of the angels—"and peace on earth to men of good will"—this was the human response.[2] The *Te Deum Laudamus*, is a Latin Christian hymn with the same theme.[3] It was written early in the fifth century by Niceta, a bishop in Dalmatia, and it, too, joins the worship of heaven to the praises of the earth. Angels, cherubim and seraphim praise the Lord with the Thrice Holy Hymn, along with the prophets, apostles, and martyrs of the past, and the whole church throughout the world. The hymn of the angels unites not only heaven and earth but also past, present, and future, time and eternity.

The prophet Enoch, whose book was Scripture for the early Christians, had similar visions of angelic worship in the holy of holies. He was taken up to heaven in his visions and saw the Lord of Hosts, surrounded by the holy and righteous ones, the saints and angels.[4] They too praised the Lord with the Thrice Holy Hymn.

Holy Holy Holy is the Lord of Spirits;

he fills the earth with spirits.

Enoch also saw the four archangels as they praised and blessed the Lord, and he himself became an angel as he joined in the worship.

In other visions Enoch saw the host of heaven praising the Creator in unison. He saw all ranks of angels—seraphim, cherubim, ophannim —dressed in white and with radiant faces, encircling the holy of holies. They must have looked like the Muslim pilgrims at Mecca as they encircle the Ka'abah. Enoch also saw that only the four archangels and the angels of the highest heaven could enter and stand before the throne of the heaven.[5]

above: **Adoration of the Magi (detail), Domenico Ghirlandaio, 1488, Italian**
The four angels who float above the stable of the nativity hold out a musical
scroll with the words "Gloria in excelsis deo," as if inviting the viewer to take
part in the song of praise to God.

The Angel Priests

The priests in the Jerusalem temple identified themselves as the angels described by Enoch, and their liturgies on earth were part of the worship of heaven. The fifth century B.C.E. prophet Malachi (whose name actually means "my angel"), described priests as angels of the Lord.[6] The high priest in the temple was the chief of the angels and so represented the Lord of Hosts on earth with his people. His outer vestment was made of the same fabric as the veil of the temple, but woven through with gold, indicating the matter of the visible world threaded through with the gold of divinity.[7] The vested angel high priest symbolized incarnation, and the vestments of a Christian priest were explained the same way. When the angel high priest emerged from the temple, the people worshiped him. Hecataeus, a Greek visitor to Jerusalem writing about 300 B.C.E., said that the Jews regarded their high priest as an angel from God. This agrees with Enoch's vision, since only the greatest angels entered the heavenly house, and only the high priest entered the holy of holies.

The Sabbath Songs among the Dead Sea Scrolls describe these angel priests as Jesus knew them. They were part of the great light of the holy of holies, their service of worship was dazzling, and the vestments of the angels were those of the priests. The figures on the walls of the temple came alive to join in the heavenly worship, and the chief of the angel priests was vested like the high priest. Other texts found among the Dead Sea Scrolls show clearly that the priests were angels who stood in eternity "illumined with perfect light for ever."

Memories of these angelic liturgies survived in the enigmatic and beautiful Jewish writings known as *Merkavah* texts. In one of these Hebrew texts known as 3 Enoch, the angels hover around the fiery throne like sparks and when they sing the Thrice Holy Hymn, the strength of the fire increases and flows out from the throne.[8] The angels who sing the hymn correctly are rewarded with crowns, but those who do not sing in perfect harmony are destroyed by a word from the throne, and new angels are created.

The first Christians modeled their worship on the angel liturgies of the Jerusalem temple. In the Book of Revelation, John described his visions of heaven. He saw the heavenly throne and the seven spirits of God, and like Isaiah, he saw the creatures with six wings who never ceased singing the Thrice Holy Hymn:

Holy Holy Holy is the Lord God Almighty,

who was and is and is to come.

As they cast down their crowns before the throne, they sang the praises of the Lord, the Creator: "For thou didst create all things, and by thy will they existed and were created."[9] John saw twenty-four elders with their golden harps and bowls of incense, and he heard the music as countless thousands in heaven joined with every creature on earth to sing before the throne of God.[10]

John saw an angel priest with a golden censer, whose smoke mingled with the prayers of the saints before God. He saw seven mighty angels with trumpets heralding the judgments on earth, but when he bowed down before a mighty angel, he was told that only God should be worshiped.[11] The angels in heaven were, like John, the servants of God. He had, however, been allowed to worship the great high priest who appeared at the beginning of his vision, the radiant figure whom he recognized as the heavenly Jesus.[12]

The ancient Greek liturgies of the Orthodox Church, which are still used today, preserve the angel worship of the Jerusalem temple. The vested priests in procession move in and out of the holy of holies, and they sing of themselves as the angelic host accompanying the Lord when he descends from heaven to earth. Narsai, a fifth-

century priest in Syria, described the holiest moment of the Christian Eucharist in words that could have come from the Dead Sea Scrolls.

In 988 C.E., Russian emissaries who visited Constantinople described the Christian worship they had seen there, they said it was so beautiful they did not know if they were on earth or in heaven. Prince Vladimir of Kiev was impressed. Later, he wanted to marry a princess of Constantinople, but as she could only marry a Christian, the Prince had Christian priests sent to baptize him, and then had all his subjects baptized. Thus the Christian faith took root in Russia because the Prince's emissaries had so marveled at the angel liturgy.

In churches of both east and west, congregations would have seen angels painted on the walls as a part of their worship, and when the vested human figures emerged from the sanctuary, they would have seemed like heavenly figures come alive. All over the Christian world, angels were often depicted as deacons, and the archangels as bishops. In the Orthodox Church, a bishop is still known as a high priest, and he still fulfills the role of the ancient angels in the temple.

The role of the angels in Christian worship is so familiar that it is often overlooked. In the Roman Catholic Mass, the priest prays that God would have his angel take the gifts from the earthly altar to the altar in heaven, so that those who received from the earthly altar would be filled with blessing from heaven. At the heart of the worship in all traditional churches, the congregations remind themselves that they are joined to the angels and archangels, and they repeat the words of the Thrice Holy Hymn first heard by Isaiah:

Holy Holy Holy, Lord God of Hosts,
Heaven and Earth are full of thy glory.

The mysteries are set in order, the censers are smoking, the lamps are shining and the deacons are hovering and waving their fans like the watching angels…
The place is filled and overflows with brightness and splendor, beauty, and power…

NARSAI, HOMILY 17A

previous page: **Angel with incense burner, stained glass**
Burning incense was a sign of priesthood, and here the angel priest brings the incense of heavenly worship.

right: **The high priest Eli questioning Samuel about his vision, engraving, mid 19th century**
The high priest was believed to be the presence of the Great Angel. In the outer part of the temple he wore colored garments to symbolize the Angel clothed in matter, incarnate, but in the holy of holies he wore white linen, the dress of angels.

And Mary said to the angel, "How shall this
be, since I have no husband?"
And the angel said to her,
"The Holy Spirit will come upon you,
and the power of the Most High will over
   shadow you;
therefore the child to be born will be called
   holy,
the Son of God.

LUKE 1, 34–35

left: **The Annunciation, Rogier van de Weyden, c. 1440, Flemish**
The priests in the Jerusalem temple were believed to be angels and the high
priest the chief of the angels. Here, the Archangel Gabriel is dressed as a
bishop. In Christian art, angels are frequently depicted in the liturgical
vestments of priests or deacons, a clear indication of the temple origins of
Christian worship.

Holy Angels, our advocates, our brothers, our counselors, our defenders, our enlighteners, our friends, our guides, our helpers, our intercessors—Pray for us.

MOTHER TERESA OF CALCUTTA

right: **Father Sergei of Radonezh conducting the Holy Liturgy, Fr. Sergei Simakov, 1989, Russian**

In a church, the sanctuary corresponds to the holy of holies in the temple, the place of the angels. The consecration of the Eucharist is also in the presence of the angels.

left and above: **Patriarchal Liturgy in the Church of the Protecting Veil of the Mother of God at Hot`kovsky Monastery near Moscow**
The procession emerging from the sanctuary with the consecrated bread and wine is the angel host that accompanies the Lord from heaven. The two deacons hold liturgical fans (rhipidia) (above right) that represent the seraphim, and so the Lord appears between two seraphim.

Interview with Abbot Silouan,

The Monastery of St. Antony and St. Cuthbert, Shropshire, England

What is the role of angels in the life of a monk or nun?

Monastic life, in the Orthodox Christian tradition, is called the angelic estate. This does not mean that monks are no longer human. It means that in their weakness and their brokenness, they are caught up into the divine love which inspires the angels, which inspires their unceasing prayer of heart, which inspires the doxology that glorifies God everywhere and in everything.

This does not happen without a profound turning around of the mind and illumination of the heart. The heart is pierced with light like a seraphic flame. The eye of the heart opens and becomes all seeing, seeing like the cherubim, all eye. The light encircles within like angelic wheels within wheels. The Kingdom of Heaven really is within us. The throne of God is within us. The sanctuary and the holy of holies are within us. To awaken to this, to realize this in our living experience, is to experience a heavenly earth and an earthly heaven. It is to be witness to paradise on earth. It is to be as the angels are. Our liturgy and their liturgy really are one liturgy. Our doxology (expression of praise to God) and their doxology are one single orthodoxy.

Orthodoxy means right glorification. It is what angels do, and what monks do, too, when they turn and awaken to God right here in the midst. Angels are not figments of the imagination or figures in an obsolete myth. We are one with them here in our midst. We are one with them in our unceasing vision and praise, invisibly but flowing over with blessing. Just as our guardian angel is said to behold the Face of God in heaven, so we on earth, with them, are caught up into vision, into light, into the glory that fills the earth and heaven in the hallowed Name.

NOTES

1 ISAIAH 6. **2** LUKE 2.14. **3** WE PRAISE THEE O GOD. **4** 1 ENOCH 49. **5** 1 ENOCH 71. **6** MALACHI 2.7. **7** EXODUS 28.6. **8** 3 ENOCH 36, 39, 40. **9** REVELATION 4. **10** REVELATION 4. **11** REVELATION 19. **12** REVELATION 1.

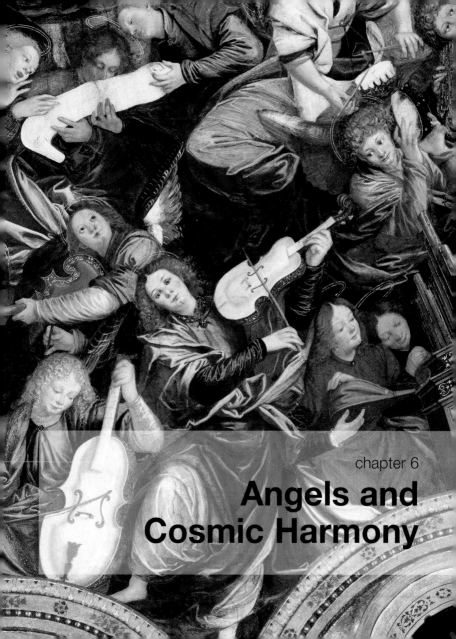

chapter 6

Angels and Cosmic Harmony

The Eternal Covenant

The Hebrew Scriptures describe the eternal covenant, a system of bonds holding all creation together. Try to imagine a multidimensional spider's web, binding all creation into one system, and everything to the Creator. If one of these bonds, or two, or even several were broken through human sin, the web was strong enough to survive. But if there was massive destruction, the whole system collapsed. Creation, human society, and individual lives just fell part. The Holy Wisdom was the great angel who bound all things together and preserved the fabric of creation intact. It was said that she kept everything in tune.

The bonds of the eternal covenant and the harmony of all creation are like the images used now by physicists in their quest for a "theory of everything." They suggest that "strings" or "superstrings" are the fundamental building blocks of the creation, and the strings vibrate in

previous page: **Musical Angels, detail of the cupola in the Sanctuary of Saronno, Gaudenzio Ferrari, 1535, Italian**
The holy of holies was the source of all life and the place of angel harmony. Psalm 150 exhorts musicians to praise the Lord in his sanctuary, with trumpets, lutes, harps, timbrels, strings, pipes, and cymbals. Angel musicians are traditionally depicted in the sanctuary of a church, which corresponds to the holy of holies.

left: **Concert of Angels, detail from the Isenheim Altarpiece, Matthias Grünewald, c. 1515, German**
This is remarkable evidence for the survival of ancient angel lore in sixteenth century Europe. Angels—no longer in nine ranks but still clearly different types—crowd the sanctuary.

different ways according to their different functions. They also predict that space-time must have more than the four dimensions of natural human experience: three of space and one of time. There are at least ten dimensions, six of them beyond our normal perception.

The angel worldview is similar. In the invisible creation, in those dimensions beyond our natural experience, which are represented by the unity of the holy of holies, the angels hold all things together, and the angels make music. Heavenly harmony is an important part of angel lore, and is the most likely origin for the widespread belief in the music of the spheres. A complex and beautiful theology was set out in terms of music and discord: the good angels make the music of creation, but the fallen angels are silent.

On his ascent through the heavens, Enoch saw the movements of the sun, moon, and stars, and heard the heavenly worship, the "marvelous singing of the angels which it is impossible to describe."[1] Then he saw the fallen angels who did not worship because they had rejected the Creator. Their faces were miserable and they did not sing.[2] When Enoch passed into an even higher heaven, he saw the archangels who arranged the music and in this way harmonized all existence in heaven and on earth.[3]

right: **Mary, Queen of Heaven, Master of the St. Lucy Legend, late 15th century, Flemish**

Mary here is depicted as Wisdom, the woman of Revelation 12, with the sun's rays at her head and the moon at her feet. As Wisdom, she holds all things in harmony, and is thus surrounded by angel musicians, many of whom are wearing vestments. Above her, the musicians of heaven play before the Trinity, and wait to receive her into their throne, when her music will join again with that of heaven. Two of the singing angels hold books with legible lyrics: "Hail Queen of Heaven," one of the ancient titles for Wisdom.

In holy music's golden speech
  Remotest notes to notes respond:
Each octave is a world; yet each
  Vibrates to worlds its own beyond.

Our narrow pale the vast resumes;
  Our sea-shell whispers of the sea:
Echoes are ours of angel-plumes
  That winnow far infinity!

AUBREY THOMAS DE VERE FROM "IMPLICIT FAITH"

right: **Glory be to God, Georgiana Houghton, 1864, British**

Houghton's spirit drawings depict the realities beyond the material world, the angel structures of the creation. She said that saints and angels helped her, and the reverse of this painting lists the names of her angel helpers and their vortex-like signatures, together with curious shapes identified as aspects of God. All these appear in the painting.

163

At last surrounds their sight
A Globe of circular light,
  That with long beams the shame-fac't night array'd,
The helmèd Cherubim
And sworded Seraphim,
  Are seen in glittering ranks with wings displaid
Harping in loud and solemn quire,
With unexpressive notes to Heav'ns new born Heir.

Such musick (as 'tis said)
Before was never made,
  But when of old the sons of morning sung,
While the Creator Great,
His constellations set,
  And the well-balanc't world on hinges hung,
And cast the dark foundations deep
And bid the weltring waves their oozy channel keep.

Ring out, ye Crystall sphears,
Once bless our human ears,
  (If ye have power to touch our senses so)
And let your silver chime
Move in melodious time;
  And let the Base of Heav'ns deep Organ blow;
And with your ninefold harmony
Make up full consort to th'Angelike symphony.

JOHN MILTON, "HYMN ON THE MORNING OF CHRIST'S NATIVITY"

left: **Dante's Vision of the Circles of Heaven, illustration to Paradiso,**
Divine Comedy, Gustave Doré, 19th century, French
The angels are the invisible part of the cosmic covenant, the web of creation
centered on God. They are the pattern of creation and their music is its harmony.

Angel Music

Angel music expressed the ideas of unity and harmony in creation, since the music was always in praise of the Creator, and acknowledged God as the Source of everything. When people on earth praised God, they joined the angel worship, committing themselves to the angels' work of harmony on earth. Music made the presence of God appear on earth, and in the temple liturgies, music was used to invite the presence of the Lord.

Even before the temple was built, King David appointed Levites to make music before the ark, to praise and thank the Lord, and to invoke his presence.[4] Jewish tradition knew of golden musical instruments in Solomon's temple; the angel priests playing there. When Solomon dedicated the temple, the musicians and singers praised the Lord "with one voice," and the Glory of the Lord filled the house.[5] Nobody knows what was meant by "one voice" but the symbolism is clear enough; music invoked the presence of the Lord.

The Jews never forgot that the Lord was present in response to human praise. The *Hekhalot Rabbati*, a Jewish mystical text perhaps from the early centuries C.E., said that the angels could only sing in response to the praises of the earth. The harmony of the visible world depended on human beings adopting the song and role of angels. Nor did they forget that the praise was continuous.[6] The *Testament of Adam* describes the continuous praises of the whole creation.

Psalm 148 describes the praise of all creation: heavens, angels, sun and moon, as well as the visible creation, but there is angel song in the Hebrew Scriptures even where angels are not mentioned. Wherever it says "the heavens rejoice," readers in the time of Jesus understood it as angels singing,[7] and so Psalm 19 is describing the praise of the angels which we cannot hear: "The heavens are telling the glory of God… Their voice is not heard." Philo, a Jewish philosopher in the first century C.E., knew that temples with their sacrifices and the music of public worship were not sufficient in themselves. The divine plan for the universe, he said, kept everything in harmony and in its appointed place, but the human contribution had to be the silent praise of a pure mind.[8]

A later legend told how Abraham ascended to heaven and saw the Holy One approaching in the sound of the angel praises. Abraham's angel guide told him to sing the fifty names of God, because he could only stand among the angels if he joined in their song.[9] When Enoch stood before the heavenly throne, he heard the people on earth singing praises as the Son of Man was given the Sacred Name.[10] At first, Enoch did not have strength to sing, but the Holy One opened his eyes and heart, so he could join in the hymn of heaven: "Holy Holy Holy."[11] If anyone unworthy heard the music, he was destroyed; and the angels who did not sing well, or who sang at the wrong times, were cast into the river of fire.[12]

Angel music was part of the process of creation, and showed its harmony. No discord was possible. The angels sang in the unity of Day One, "with one voice, with one speech, with one knowledge and with one sound."[13] In Isaiah's temple vision in 742 B.C.E., the earliest reference to cosmic song, the seraphim sang of the Glory filling the whole earth. The morning stars sang as the foundations of the earth were put in place,[14] and temple musicians had to sing a "new/renewing" song as the Lord created heaven and earth.[15] Angel music was often associated with healing and renewal, re-creation. There is a "new/renewing" song in Psalm 144, where the Lord brings victory and new prosperity, another in Isaiah 42 when the Lord transforms the creation and restores his people.

Then I saw the lucent sky, in which I heard different kinds of music, marvelously embodying all the meanings I had heard before. I heard the praises of the joyous citizens of heaven, steadfastly persevering in the ways of truth; and laments calling people back to those praises and joys…

HILDEGARD OF BINGEN, VISION THIRTEEN

right: **Sacred Music, Luigi Mussini, 1841, Italian**

Angels exist to praise God, and they look up toward God, the Source of all as they sing. Holding music indicates that an angel is singing.

Angels we have heard on high
Sweetly singing o'er the plains,
And the mountains in reply
Echoing their joyous strains:
Gloria in excelsis Deo,
Gloria in excelsis Deo.

ANONYMOUS, "ANGELS WE HAVE HEARD ON HIGH,"
TRADITIONAL ENGLISH CAROL

left: **Angel Musicians (detail), Hans Memling, 15th century, Flemish**
Angel musicians, wearing various types of church vestments, recall the role of
the priests and Levites in Solomon's temple, who had golden instruments to
make music and invoke the presence of the Lord on earth.

following page: **The Mystic Nativity (detail), Sandro Botticelli, 1501, Italian**
Just as Enoch had a vision of the angels encircling the holy of holies with their
songs of praise, so here, the place of Christ's birth has become the new holy of
holies and the angels dance and sing their praises on earth.

He divided light from obscurity, he established the dawn by the knowledge of his heart. When all his angels saw it, they sang, for he showed them that which they had not known.

DEAD SEA SCROLLS 11Q5

right: **When the Morning Stars Sang Together, illustration to the *Book of Job*, William Blake, 1805–06, British**

The Lord spoke to Job from the whirlwind and asked him—here shown with his wife and three counselors—if he been at the beginning of all things, when the Morning Stars sang as the earth was set in place, and the sons of God rejoiced. Here the cosmic music is covered by the cloud, and God is accompanied by two other angel figures: the male Logos, who is a horseman, and the female Wisdom, leading away Leviathan.

Look, how the floor of heaven
Is thick inlaid with patines of bright gold:
There's not the smallest orb which thou behold'st
But in his motion like an angel sings,
Still quiring to the young-eyed cherubins;
Such harmony is in immortal souls;
But, whilst this muddy vesture of decay
Doth grossly close it in, we cannot hear it.

WILLIAM SHAKESPEARE, *THE MERCHANT OF VENICE*, ACT 5

left: **Christ Glorified in the Court of Heaven (detail), Fra Angelico,
1423–24, Italian**
The angels rejoice because Christ has been raised from the dead and returned
to heaven, to the center of cosmic harmony.

On Earth as it is in Heaven

When St. John had a vision of heaven, he heard music. He heard the song of re-creation, when the highest ranks of heaven praised the One who created all things and continues to create.[16] At the heart of the creation, the powers of heaven were praising the Source of Life:

> Worthy art thou, our Lord and God, to receive Glory and Honor and Power,
>
> For Thou didst create all things, and by Thy will they existed and were created.

Once the Lamb, the human, had been restored to the throne above the angel powers, all the visible creation joined with the invisible in a chorus of praise. Heaven, as the first Christians knew it, was a place of music, and so music was an important part of their worship.[17] "On earth as it is in heaven" was used to describe the music of the churches as they restored the harmony of heaven and earth.

Because the angels were a unity in heaven, Christian music showed their unity and harmony on earth. Paul wrote to the Christians at Colossae that they should have an angel lifestyle, holy and loving in perfect harmony, and singing psalms and hymns.[18]

Gregory, bishop of Nyssa,[19] explained in a Christmas sermon that the whole creation was the temple of the Creator, but that sin had come in and silenced the praise. The human creation no longer joined the song of the angels. When Christ restored sinners, angels and humans were once again united in their praise. Maximus the Confessor,[20] one of the great teachers of the Eastern Church, taught that Christians singing was a sign they had become angels. Christian souls, he said, having become equal in dignity with the angels, joined in their praises. In the age to come, heaven and earth would enjoy the same way of life, and be part of the same harmony of divine praise.[21]

above: **The Mormon Tabernacle Choir, Salt Lake City, 1974**

The Saints on earth join their songs with the Saints and Angels in heaven.

right: **St. Cecilia playing the spinet, with angel, Orazio Gentileschi, early 17th century, Italian**

St. Cecilia was a martyr of the Roman church, venerated as early as the fourth century C.E. When the Academy of Music was founded in Rome in 1584, she was made its patron, and is now the patron saint of church music. She is usually depicted with an organ, but here an angel teaches her to play the spinet.

Interview with Fr. Robert Murray, S.J.

Heythrop College, University of London

What part do angels play in the lives of Catholic Christians today?

All Catholics are brought up on the Bible stories of angelic appearances, especially the Annunciation to Mary, the angel strengthening Jesus in his agony and St. Michael's victory over the forces of evil. In the catechism, all Catholics learn about the existence and nature of angels, and that each person has a guardian angel for whose help and protection it is good to pray.

Angels figure importantly in the liturgy of the Mass, especially in the prefaces to the central Eucharistic prayer. Catholics grow up with a strong sense that angels invisibly lead the congregation's worship at Mass and in services of adoration. This is all firm Catholic tradition, which is seen to remain solid in the greater part of worldwide Catholicism. In Asia, Africa, and Latin America, belief in angels is well to the fore, doubtless still fed by compatible and deep roots in traditional religion.

In Western Europe and North America, the last century has seen an apparent decline in active belief in angels after childhood, doubtless under secular influences dominating in education; but this is less true for those who have absorbed less of those influences. Even among the few who study Aquinas for philosophy of religion, probably hardly any are aware that the hierarchy of angels forms the very backbone of his whole cosmology.

However, some leading Catholic thinkers and writers find new and creative ways to renew faith in angels and their significance for humanity. Most strikingly, J. R. R. Tolkien's imaginary history of "Middle Earth" starts with the supreme being "Iluvatar," who, having created the "Ainur" ("Holy Ones"), proposes music for them to develop. One of these, Melkor, rebelliously creates discord but this is overcome by richer harmony. Iluvatar reveals the music's meaning, as the whole future world of living beings of various natures, all created good but with one higher power of evil continuing. Some of the Ainur, called "Valar" ("Powers") descend to earth to lead and protect humans and the other created races in the war against evil. The Valar have attendant spirits who are mortal but able to rise again to new life, among whom are the "Istari" (wizards), including Gandalf (good) and Saruman until he is corrupted by the enemy. Tolkien made it clear in letters (now published) that his imaginary beings partly reflect his belief in angels.

NOTES

1 2 ENOCH 17. **2** 2 ENOCH 18. **3** 2 ENOCH 19. **4** 1 CHRONICLES 16.4. **5** 2 CHRONICLES 5.
6 1 CHRONICLES 16.37. **7** E.G. THE TARGUM TO 1 CHRONICLES 16.31. **8** ON PLANTING 10, 126.
9 APOCALYPSE OF ABRAHAM 17. **10** 1 ENOCH 48. **11** 3 ENOCH 1. **12** 3 ENOCH 47.
13 HEKHALOT RABBATI, 185. **14** JOB 38. **15** PSALM 33. **16** REVELATION 4. **17** EPHESIANS 5.
18 COLOSSIANS 3. **19** DIED 395CE. **20** DIED 662CE. **21** MYSTAGOGY 23-24

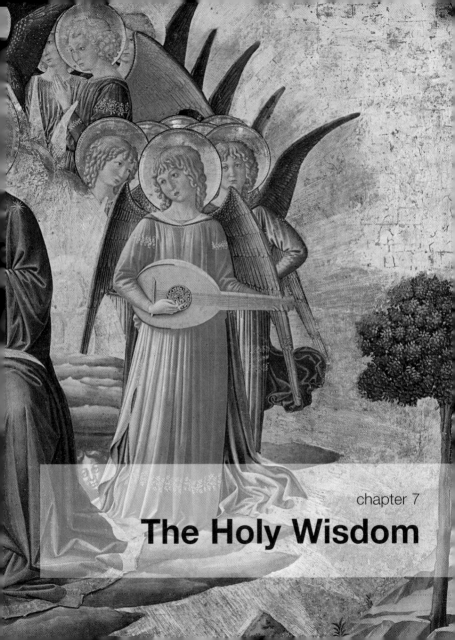

chapter 7

The Holy Wisdom

The Lost Lady

The Holy Wisdom is one of the great angels. Many cathedrals of the Eastern Orthodox Church are dedicated to her, and she appears in some of their most mysterious icons. She sits on a throne within rings of light, a winged, fiery figure, dressed in white, carrying a scroll and a staff. But who is she? One of her symbols was the Tree of Life, remembered as a fragrant, fiery tree.[1] In the temple this has been represented by the seven branched lamp, which had been made like a golden tree.[2]

Wisdom is mentioned in the Book of Proverbs. She spoke to her people like a goddess—"I will pour out my spirit to you; I will make my words known to you."[3] Her name could have a plural form—a sure sign of divinity— giving her devotees life and true wealth, honor, peace, and happiness.[4] She had been present at the creation, "brought forth"—the Hebrew word implies birth—before the mountains and the seas were formed.[5] Who was Wisdom, born before the visible creation, a divine being in the holy of holies, an angel in the Source of life?

The poem in Proverbs 8 also describes her as the one who joins together, or the one who holds in harmony. Since one role of the angels was to make connections between different aspects of human perception—to "inspire"—Wisdom had a special place at the head of the angels, holding them all together. They were her children, and by their work enabled Wisdom to permeate the creation.

previous page: **The Madonna Giving Her Girdle to St. Thomas, Bernazzo Gozzoli, 1450, Italian**
Many pictures of Mary depict her as the Holy Wisdom. Here she is enthroned in heaven, surrounded by the angels who represent her harmony.

Human beings were created in the image of God, "male and female," so there must be male-and-female in the Creator, and Wisdom is the female aspect.[6] Here we have the problem of words, since there can be no "he" or "she" in the state of the bodiless powers, but these distinctions are necessary in the material world where humans experience the powers. Hebrew has no neuter—there was no "it"—and so in Genesis the Creator was male and female. The assumption that we speak of everything divine as "he" has caused huge distortions in theology, and the Holy Wisdom is a stark reminder of something long neglected.

Jeremiah described people in Jerusalem and Judaea who had worshiped the Queen of Heaven.[7] They had fled as refugees to Egypt after the fall of Jerusalem in 586 B.C.E., and refused to accept what the prophet told them: that worshiping the Queen of Heaven had caused the disaster. They argued that she had protected Jerusalem, and when her worshipers abandoned her, she abandoned them and their city. These refugees and their descendents did not abandon Wisdom and preserved the traditions about her.

There is a similar account in 1 Enoch 93, that just before the temple was destroyed, the priests forsook Wisdom and thus lost their vision. Wisdom returned to heaven and took her place among the angels.[8] The Queen of Heaven was one of the titles for Wisdom, who had been rejected by the religious leaders in Jerusalem, but not by the rest of the people. One of her gifts to the priests had been "vision," and with her departure, their spiritual eyes were closed. The vision they lost was the world of the angels. The religious leaders who made these changes in the seventh century B.C.E. taught that the "secret things"—the world of the angels—belonged to the Lord alone. They were no concern of ordinary people who had only to obey the ten commandments.[9]

Ezekiel, a temple priest who prophesied at this time, actually described Wisdom leaving the temple. His strange visions of the chariot throne of the Lord leaving the temple,[10] include a winged, fiery female figure, sometimes singular, sometimes plural. She usually appears in English translations as the "Living Creatures," but Ezekiel also described her as "the Living One." She was set within two great circles of lights—usually translated as "a wheel within a wheel" and "full of eyes."[11]

The figure in Ezekiel's vision is very likely the Holy Wisdom depicted, centuries later, in the most ancient Russian icons. People had not forgotten Wisdom, the Living One, the Queen of Heaven. Christian hymns to Mary in the seventh century C.E. also used Wisdom images: she was described as the chariot of the Lord and the fiery throne.

When there were no depths, I was brought forth,
When there were no springs abounding with water.
Before the mountains had been shaped,
Before the hills, I was brought forth...
When he marked the foundations of the earth,
I was beside him like a master workman.

PROVERBS 8. 24-5, 29-30

above: **The Creation of Man (detail), Sistine Chapel ceiling, Vatican, Rome, Michelangelo, 1510, Italian**

According to Proverbs 8, Wisdom was beside the Creator as He worked. Here, she is the female figure in the crook of the Creator's arm.

Happy is the person who finds Wisdom, the person who
  gets understanding,
For the gain from her is better than from silver, and profit
  from her better than gold.
She is more precious than jewels, and nothing you desire
  can compare with her.
Long life is in her right hand; in her left are riches and
  honor.
Her ways are ways of pleasantness, and all her paths are
  peace.
She is a tree of life to those who lay hold of her
Those who hold her fast are called happy.

PROVERBS 3

left: **Sophia, Angel of Wisdom, icon, Novgorod, Russian traditional**
Icons of the Holy Wisdom are the most mysterious in the Church's tradition.
They represent an almost forgotten theology, which was important when they
were painted and when great cathedrals were dedicated to her. Here, the Holy
Wisdom is a fiery angel like the figure in Ezekiel's vision, crowned and enthroned
beneath a starry firmament. She is encircled by a wheel within a wheel of light,
and on either side of her are John the Baptist and Mary. The throne in heaven is
empty because the Lord appears above the Holy Wisdom.

following page: **Madonna and Child enthroned, with Angels and Saints,
the San Barnaba Altarpiece (detail), Sandro Botticelli, c. 1490, Italian**
The angels are bodiless powers, and do not have the gender distinctions we
need. Artists try to depict an angel as neither male nor female.

Wisdom the High Priest

Wisdom was remembered as the angel high priest in the temple in Jerusalem—Ezekiel had described a cherub high priest in the Garden of God.[13] She had been the perfumed anointing oil that had transformed the kings and high priests into angels, and the Tree of Life, whose fruit gave Wisdom.[14] Descendants of the refugees in Egypt said it was Wisdom who had protected Noah, guided Abraham and inspired Moses,[15] even though the Hebrew Scriptures say it was the Lord who did this. Thus the guardian angel of Israel could be described as the Lord or as Wisdom, male or female, and when that angel was incarnate in Jesus, St. Paul could speak of Jesus as the Power of God (male) and the Wisdom of God (female).[16]

In the Book of Revelation, Jesus in heaven dictated seven letters to John, and in the one to Laodicea he described himself as Wisdom—so there are no gender distinctions in heaven. He said he was the Amon, a Hebrew title for Wisdom which means "the craftsman."[17] In the Greek Old Testament it became "the woman who joins all things together" or "who keeps things in tune." The rest of the letter described Wisdom's other gifts: true wealth, the white garments of heavenly Life, and eyes with vision.[18]

Wisdom was also known as the Angel of Great Counsel. When the king in Jerusalem was anointed, he was thought of as an angel, a child of Wisdom, and Isaiah described the angels' song when he was "born": "Unto us a child is born, unto us a son is given."[19] He was given four titles: "Wonderful Counselor, Mighty God, Everlasting Father, Prince of Peace," but the Greek version had just one: "The Angel of Great Counsel."

From eternity, in the beginning, he created me,
And for eternity I shall not cease to exist.
In the holy tabernacle I ministered before him,
And so I was established in Zion.
In the beloved city likewise he gave me a resting place.
And in Jerusalem was my dominion.

BEN SIRA 24.9–11

left: **Madonna of Humility, School of Padua, 16th century, Italian**
Mary, the pregnant Virgin, is already a heavenly figure because she is the
earthly counterpart of the Holy Wisdom. Here she has her retinue of angels,
and shelters her earthly children under her protecting veil. She joins heaven
and earth.

And a great sign appeared in heaven, a woman clothed with the sun, with the moon under her feet, and on her head a crown of twelve stars; she was with child and she cried out in her pangs of birth, in anguish for delivery. And another portent appeared in heaven; behold, a great red dragon, with seven heads and ten horns, and seven diadems upon his heads. His tail swept down a third of the stars of heaven, and cast them to the earth. And the dragon stood before the woman who was about to bear a child, that he might devour her child when she brought it forth; she brought forth a male child, one who is to rule all the nations with a rod of iron, but her child was caught up to god and to his throne, and the woman fled into the wilderness, where she had a place prepared by God, in which to be nourished for one thousand two hundred and sixty days.

REVELATION 12

right: **Woman clothed in the sun, from the Beatus of Liébana (Silos Apocalypse), 1109, Spanish**

St. John saw a sign in heaven. A woman clothed with the sun and crowned with stars emerged to give birth to her child. She was the Queen of Heaven—another of Wisdom's titles—the virgin whom Isaiah said would give birth to the Messiah.

pugnana

duodecim

serpens

Around her you see a beautiful multitude, with the appearance and wings of angels, standing in great veneration, for they both fear and love her. Which is to say that all the blessed and excellent spirits in the heavenly ministry worship the knowledge of God with inexpressibly pure praise, as humans cannot worthily do, while they are in their mortal bodies. These spirits embrace God in their ardour, for they are living light; and they are winged, not in the sense that they have wings like flying creatures, but in the sense that they circle burningly in their spheres through the power of God, as if they were winged.

HILDEGARD OF BINGEN, *SCIVIAS* 3.4.16

right: **The Virgin and the Angels, Adolphe William Bouguereau, 1900, French**

Enoch said that Wisdom was seated in heaven in the midst of the heavenly host. Here Mary is depicted as Wisdom, the Queen of heaven and the angel priests offer her incense, a sign that she is divine. She is crowned with stars and set with her child in the midst of the angels.

The Mother

Wisdom was also the Mother of the Lord. The virgin whom Isaiah said would bear the child Immanuel, "God with us," must have been Wisdom, the Queen of Heaven.[20] She was also the unnamed woman in Micah's prophecy, who would bear the great shepherd of Israel.[21] Shortly after the time of Isaiah and Micah, she was rejected, and returned to heaven to take her place among the angels.[22]

She reappeared in John's vision, when there was a great sign in heaven. First the ark appeared in the holy of holies, and then a woman clothed with the sun and crowned with stars, the Queen of Heaven. She gave birth to a son who was taken up to God's throne, escaping the red dragon waiting to devour him.[23] The woman then took to her wings and fled into the desert to escape the dragon. This was the angel Mother of the Man who sat on the throne of God, and so the first Christians must have been expecting Wisdom to return and give birth to her son.

When the early Christians told the story of Mary, they depicted her as Wisdom. There is no other way to explain the imagery in the Infancy Gospel of James, which was in use by the mid second century and could be even older. Mary was offered to the temple as a child and grew up there, just like the infant Samuel.[24] She was fed by an angel, presumably by a priest. She played in the temple and everyone was

left: **Presentation of the Virgin Mary in the Temple, icon, 16th century, Russian**

The Infancy Gospel of James tells the life story of Mary using many Wisdom motifs. This icon depicts two scenes: Mary taken to the temple as a child, and then being fed by an angel in the holy of holies, which is traditionally shown as a canopy with four pillars. This story also appears in the Koran.

Hail for you reveal the angels' way of life,
Hail, tree of glorious fruit from which believers are
   nourished,
Hail, wood with shady leaves under which many shelter.

Hail, all holy chariot of him who rides upon the Cherubim
Hail, best of dwellings of him who is above the Seraphim,
Hail for you bring opposites to harmony...

We see the Holy Virgin as a lamp that bears the light
Shining for those in darkness.
For kindling the immaterial Light she guides all to divine
knowledge, enlightening the mind by its ray...

FROM ORTHODOX CHURCH'S *AKATHIST HYMN* TO MARY

left: **The Virgin of the Burning Bush, icon, 19th century, Russian**
This is Wisdom imagery used for Mary and the Child, who are in the midst of
symbols of the holy of holies: seraphim, angels of the weathers and the four
living creatures. Mary is clothed with cloud, just as Wisdom had appeared in a
pillar of cloud. The eight-pointed star is another Wisdom symbol, where the red
zone represents the fire of the burning bush and the green the bush itself. In the
older temple tradition, the red was the fiery living creatures, and the green was
the emerald rainbow round the throne of heaven. Later Jewish mystics
remembered the green zone as the source of time, the depth of the divine glory
and the ancient Wisdom.

delighted, just as in Proverbs, Wisdom had been the Creator's delight, playing before him in the world.[25] When Mary reached puberty, she left the temple, and the priests found a husband for her. Then she was chosen to help weave a new veil for the temple, and while she was spinning, an angel of the Lord told her she would be the Mother of the Son of God. This is depicted in every icon of the Annunciation that shows Mary spinning red wool.

When the Christians composed hymns in honor of Mary, they used images of Wisdom. She was "the fragrant incense and myrrh of great price;" she was "the Tree with glorious fruit from which believers are nourished;" she was "the Lampstand," or "the one who enlightens many with knowledge." St. Justin Martyr, a Christian teacher in the mid second century, explained that the angel of the Lord who spoke to Moses in the Burning Bush had many names.[26] He was "The Glory of the Lord, the Son, Wisdom, the Angel, the Lord,"[27] and Mary, too, was described as the "burning bush," which had been "burned with fire but not consumed." Perhaps Mary as the burning bush was a memory of Wisdom's fiery Tree of Life.

Mary is often depicted as the Holy Wisdom, sometimes even dressed as a high priest. She may be in the apse of a church, which corresponds to the holy of holies, or surrounded by the weather angels of Day One in a type of icon known as "the burning bush." She may be enthroned with her Son in heaven, surrounded by the cherubim of knowledge, or surrounded by the musicians of cosmic harmony. Or she may be simply enthroned as the Queen of Heaven.

NOTES

1 2 ENOCH 8. **2** EXODUS 25 **3** PROVERBS 1. **4** PROVERBS 3. **5** PROVERBS 8. **6** GENESIS 1.
7 JEREMIAH 24. **8** 1 ENOCH 42. **9** DEUTERONOMY 29. **10** EZEKIEL 1 & 10. **11** EZEKIEL 10.
12 THE AKATHIST HYMN. **13** EZEKIEL 28. **14** BEN SIRA 24. **15** WISDOM OF SOLOMON 10.
16 1 CORINTHIANS 1. **17** PROVERBS 8. **18** REVELATION 3. **19** ISAIAH 9. **20** ISAIAH 7.
21 MICAH 5. **22** 1 ENOCH 42. **23** REVELATION 12. **24** 1 SAMUEL 2. **25** PROVERBS 8.
26 EXODUS 3. **27** TRYPHO 60.

chapter 8
The Fallen Angels

Lost Angels

There are no stories about fallen angels in the Bible, but many passages suggest that such stories were known. Genesis has a short story about "sons of God" taking human wives and bringing great wickedness to the earth, but for the full story we have to look in 1 Enoch. This book is not in most Bibles today, but it was Scripture for the first Christians, and remained in the Bible of the ancient Church of Ethiopia. When St. Paul described the corrupted creation waiting for the (new) sons of God,[1] he was thinking of this story of the fallen angels. When St. John saw a red dragon bringing one third of the stars down to earth, and then saw St. Michael and his angels fighting against them,[2] and when he saw an angel binding Satan and locking him in a bottomless pit for a thousand years,[3] these were visions of the fallen angels.

St. John may have been thinking of the story in 1 Enoch, or it may have been the story of Lucifer, the proud Day Star described by Isaiah, who was thrown from heaven because he tried to make himself greater than God. Isaiah warned the king of Babylon that he was behaving like Lucifer and would also be cast down. The man who aspired to set his throne above the stars of God, he said, would be brought down to Sheol, the place of the dead, and his sons would die.[4] Isaiah also knew the Enoch story because he described the rebel sons of God and the offspring of evildoers, who had brought corruption to the earth.[5] He described them as stars, so he must have believed that the stars were alive, and he knew that the rebel stars/angels in heaven would be punished together with the rebel kings on earth. He thought that great stars/angels acted through human kings, which explains why the wise men in the Christmas story knew a great king had been born when they saw a new star in the sky.[6]

previous page: **Fall of the Rebel Angels, Pieter Bruegel (the Elder), 1562, Flemish**

In the world of the angels, unnatural forms and monsters always represent evil. Here the demon offspring of the fallen angels are driven into the great pit and bound in the depths of the earth to await the Day of Judgment. The light and order of St. Michael and his angels contrasts with the darkness and disorder of the evil ones. The circle of light at the top of the picture suggests the mouth of the great pit.

above: **St. Michael and his angels fighting the dragon, from the Revelations of St. John (Douce Apocalypse), 13th century, English**

Let triumph "the better angels of our nature."

ABRAHAM LINCOLN

left: **Abdeil leads the good Angels to fight with Satan, illustration to** *Paradise Lost*, **Gustave Doré, 1866, French**

Evil is the greatest problem for any religion which believes in the unity of God, and that God is good. If God is the all-powerful Creator, God cannot be good; or, if God is good, God cannot be all powerful. Evil was explained as the result of war in heaven, which affected the earth. Satan rebelled against God, but when he and his angels were defeated in heaven, they determined to corrupt the earth in revenge. Human sin was the result of their evil influence. Satan was the great deceiver, and the real battle was for the human mind.

Lucifer: As it is, I know
Something of pity. When I reeled in Heaven,
And my sword grew too heavy for my grasp,
Stabbing through matter, which it could not pierce
So much as the first shell of,—toward the throne;
When I fell back, down,—staring up as I fell,—
The lightnings holding open my scathed lids,
And that thought of the infinite of God,
Hurled after to precipitate descent;
When countless angel faces still and stern
Pressed out upon me from the level heavens
Adown the abysmal spaces, and I fell
Trampled down by your stillness, and struck blind
By the sight within your eyes,—'twas then I knew
How ye could pity, my kind angelhood!

ELIZABETH BARRETT BROWNING, *A DRAMA OF EXILE*

right: **Archangel Michael in combat with Lucifer, Antonio Maria Viani, late 16th century, Italian**

Lucifer was originally a name for the planet Venus, the Morning Star. In the Latin Vulgate Bible, to rise like Lucifer is a sign of hope. He was obedient to the Lord and rose at his command each morning. Isaiah 14 describes him as a proud heavenly being who had tried to set his throne above the throne of God, and St. Jerome, explaining this, said that Lucifer was the principal fallen angel, who had lost his glory as the Morning Star. Early Christian teachers said Lucifer was not the name of the devil, but a reminder of the glorious state from which he had fallen.

The Rebel Angels

Parts of 1 Enoch are ancient stories about angels, for example how Azazel and Semhaza made a solemn bond with 200 angels and came to earth. They lusted for human women, and came to earth where they taught people how to work metals into weapons; how to make cosmetics and jewelry, which led to fornication; how to use drugs and kill an unborn child; how to work magic and read the stars and clouds.[7] Their children were the demons who infested the earth.

These rebels against God abused their heavenly knowledge for evil ends, causing much wickedness and bloodshed on earth. Four archangels were sent to help their victims: Uriel warned Noah of the flood to come, Gabriel destroyed the demon children of the fallen angels, Raphael imprisoned Azazel, and Michael imprisoned Semhaza. They would be bound for seventy generations, so that the earth could be healed and restored to fertility. When Enoch went on his heavenly journey, he saw the abyss of fire which was their prison.

1 Enoch shows there was an ancient Hebrew tradition about angels, their fall, and their judgment. The angels were the powers of creation, and in a way we no longer understand, had and *were* knowledge about the creation. They were bonds, and enabled humans to see and know the creation, to make connections and see the whole. When the angel knowledge was cut off from its source and used in rebellion against God, "The Great Holy One," the earth became as fragmented as the knowledge. In biblical language, the bonds of the eternal covenant were broken, and everything fell apart. The Greek word for devil is *diabolos*, which means the one who misrepresents: "That ancient serpent who is called the Devil and Satan, the deceiver of the whole world."[8] Those who came under the power of the fallen angels lost their spiritual sight. This was the exact

opposite of Wisdom who held all things together and gave vision. When Jesus opened the eyes of the blind, these were more than miracles; they were signs of conquering evil angels.

Enoch told the history of Israel,[9] but he did not mention Eve being tempted in the Garden of Eden. For him, evil came into the world only when the stars/angels fell from heaven.[10] Elsewhere we read of five Satans—"adversaries"—who tempted humans to do evil: Yeqon, the first Satan, led the angels astray, Asbeel, the second, lured them to lust, Gadriel led Eve astray, Penemue taught writing and Kasdeya taught abortion.

In the Hebrew Scriptures there is only an unnamed Satan who tempted the Lord to test his servant Job,[11] an unnamed Satan who tried to accuse the high priest Joshua,[12] and an unnamed Satan who tempted King David to sin.[13] In the New Testament, Satan tempted Jesus to doubt that he was the Son of God,[14] spoke through Peter to tempt Jesus away from his path of suffering,[15] and finally worked through Judas Iscariot to have Jesus arrested.[16] In the Book of Revelation, Satan was "the Devil, the ancient serpent, and the red dragon;"[12] his agent on earth was the beast from the sea,[18] and men worshiped him. An angel bound him in a pit for a thousand years, and after the final battle, he was thrown into the lake of fire.[19]

The literature and legends about Dr. Faustus are European versions of this fallen angels myth, based on the story of a sixteenth-century magician. Dr. Faustus wanted all knowledge because it would give him all power. He promised his soul to the devil when he died, if he could have all the magical power he wanted while he was alive. He was prepared to abandon God in return for knowledge and power, but in the end, the devil claimed him and took him to eternal punishment.

Then the devil taketh him up into the holy city, and setteth him on a pinnacle of the temple,
And saith unto him, If Thou be the Son of God, cast thyself down: for it is written, He shall give his angels charge concerning thee: and in their hands they shall bear thee up, lest at any time thou dash thy foot against a stone.
Jesus said unto him, It is written again, Thou shalt not tempt the Lord thy God.
Again, the devil taketh him up an exceeding high mountain, and sheweth him all the kingdoms of the world, and the glory of them;
And saith unto him, All these things will I give thee, if thou wilt fall down and worship me.

MATTHEW 4.5–11

right: **Temptation of Christ on the Mountain, from the Maesta Altarpiece, Duccio di Buoninsegna, c. 1308–11, Italian**
At his baptism in the River Jordan, Jesus heard the heavenly voice saying, "Thou are my Son." This is a quotation from Psalm 2, which promises that the Son will be given the nations and the ends of the earth. After his baptism, Jesus went into the desert and must have been meditating on this Psalm. He felt the devil taking him up to a high place and promising him all the kingdoms of the earth. All Jesus had to do was worship the devil, a reference to the story of Satan's expulsion, who had been thrown from heaven because he refused to worship Adam, the Image of God. Satan had been created first, and so Adam should worship him. Here Jesus, the Second Adam, relived that old conflict.

Mephistopheles:
I am the price that all things pay for being,
The shadow on the world, thrown by the world
Standing in its own light, which light God is.
So first, when matter was, I was called Change,
And next, when life began, I was called Pain,
And last, when knowledge was, I was called Evil;
Nothing myself, except to give a name
To these three values, Permanence, Pleasure, Good,
The Godward side of matter life and knowledge.

DOROTHY L. SAYERS, *THE DEVIL TO PAY*

left: **Faust and Mephistopheles making their pact, illustration to Goethe's *Faust*, early 20th century**

Christopher Marlowe wrote his play *Dr. Faustus* about 1590, based on the life of the German scholar and magician who had died in 1541. Goethe's Faust is a more elaborate tale, incorporating elements from the Book of Job. Mephistopheles bargains with God for the soul of Faust and God permits him to try to lead Faust astray. Faust's greatest desire was for knowledge, and he was tricked into a pact by Mephistopheles: knowledge and success in return for his soul. The complex tale culminates with Faust trying to redesign the creation and create his own earth, but he becomes blind. As he dies, Mephistopheles comes to claim his soul, but angels rescue him and take his soul to heaven.

What animal is this that coils and winds
His oblique course toward me? How he rears
Aloft his scaly mottled head: and forth
Launches his triple tongue: his glittering eye
Glares with indescribable fire, that burns
And scintillates, and seems to scorch my soul
With horrible fascination.

HUGO GROTIUS, *ADAMUS EXUL*

right: **Adam and Eve Expelled from Paradise, and the Birth of Death,
illustration to St. Augustine's City of God, 1486–1587**

St. Augustine, in his City of God, said that Adam and Eve were tempted by the
snake to become more than they were, and thus became less. God allowed
humans to keep what they had chosen. Having aspired to be independent of
God, they found they were living a dissatisfied life, in perpetual bondage to the
evil one whose words they had believed. They had chosen spiritual death when
they disobeyed God, and this led to physical death. They were condemned to
eternal death because they had forsaken eternal life. In the Book of Revelation,
this pattern is reversed; the Lord promises the faithful Christians that they will
again be allowed to eat from the tree of life.

Satan Thrown from Heaven

There are other versions of the Lucifer story in the Life of Adam and Eve and the Apocalypse of Moses. All the angels were created on Day One, and when Adam was created as the Image of God, Michael summoned all the angels to worship the Image. Satan refused. Adam should worship him, said Satan, because he had been created first. For his pride and disobedience, God drove Satan and his angels from heaven and cast them to earth. Deprived of their original place in glory, Satan and his horde determined to take revenge on Adam. God had appointed two angels to guard the human pair in Eden, but when it was time for the angels to worship God, Satan seized his opportunity. Disguised as an angel of light, and singing hymns of praise to God, he leaned over the wall of the garden. He persuaded Eve to open the gate to him, and once inside, convinced her to take the forbidden fruit and give some to Adam.

Michael and the angels then returned with the Lord to Eden. The cherub throne was set by the Tree of Life, and the guilty pair were summoned and sentenced. The angels drove them from the garden, but they granted Adam one wish: he was allowed to take the seeds to grow food, and seeds to grow fragrant plants for incense. Thus he could recreate the perfume of Eden, and have incense to offer with his prayers so that God would hear him. When he was dying, Adam sent Eve and Seth back to Eden, to see if God would allow him some oil from the Tree of life and thus save him from death, but Michael said the oil would be given again only in the last days. When Adam died, the heavenly chariot came for him, accompanied by a throng of seraphim and angels with incense. They prayed for God's mercy on Adam, and then Michael took him to the third heaven to wait for the Day of Judgment.

This story of Satan's envy and fall was well known to the first Christians. St. Paul said Satan could disguise himself as an angel of light.[20] Jesus alluded to this story when describing his own experiences. In the wilderness, Satan offered Jesus all the kingdoms of the world, if he would worship him, recalling Satan's original claim that the image of God should worship him. Jesus saw Satan fall like lightning from heaven,[21] recalling how Satan was thrown down when Adam triumphed. The writer to the Hebrews knew the angels had to worship the Son.[22] St. John saw the Son enthroned in heaven, with Satan and his angels cast to earth,[23] and the great conflict with evil was the dark counterpart of this story. Just as the Lord had breathed life into Adam, his image, and commanded all the angels to worship him, so too the beast had breathed life into his image, and commanded everyone to worship it on pain of death.[24] This story of the fall of Satan is also found in the Koran,[25] and was almost certainly used by John Milton (1608–74) as a source for his epic poem *Paradise Lost*.

Satan was known by many names. In Jewish texts from the first century B.C.E., he was known as Prince Mastema, and in the Dead Sea Scrolls, he was called Belial, Melchiresa', the Angel of Perdition, and the Prince of the kingdom of wickedness. He had three names, apparently, but the text is so broken that we cannot decipher the third name. In the New Testament he was called Belial, the ancient serpent and the Deceiver.[26] In other early Christian texts he was called Sammael, meaning "the blind god"—because he had lost his spiritual vision—Beliar or Belial, and Malkira', meaning the king of evil. Melchiresa' or Malkira' has exactly the opposite meaning to Melchizedek, a title given to Jesus:[27] "My king is evil" and "My king is righteous." Jesus was depicted as exactly the opposite to the fallen, rebel angel, the Deceiver; he was the obedient Servant who saw the Truth.

Six things are said respecting demons. In three particulars they are like angels, and in three they resemble men. They have wings like angels, like angels they fly from one end of the world to the other, and they know the future, as angels do, with this difference, that they learn by listening behind the veil what angels have revealed to them within. In three respects they resemble men: They eat and drink like men, they beget and increase like men, and like men they die.

TALMUD *CHAGIGAH* 16

right: **Satan smitten by Michael, from *Paradise Lost*, Gustave Doré, 1866, French**

In John Milton's *Paradise Lost*, the archangel Raphael told Adam the story of Satan's fall, before the the visible world had been created. In Book 6 he described the great battle waged by Michael and Gabriel and their army against the host of Satan. Michael and Satan met in single combat and Satan was wounded in his right. "Nectarous humor" flowed from the wound—angels do not have blood—but Satan was rescued by his followers and carried on their shields back to his chariot. Eventually the Messiah intervenes in the battle, drives Satan out and returns in triumph to heaven. Here, Satan is depicted with his wounded side, waiting to be rescued by his angels.

225

Satan, so call him now, his former name
Is heard no more in heav'n; he of the first
If not the first Arch-Angel, great in Power,
In favour and pre-eminence, yet fraught
With envy against the Son of God, that day
Honour'd by his great Father, and proclaim'd
Messiah King anointed, could not bear
Through pride that sight, and thought himself impair'd.
Deep malice thus conceiving and disdain,
Soon as midnight brought on the dusky hour
Friendliest to sleep and silence, he resolv'd
With all his legions to dislodge, and leave
Unworshipt, unobeyed the Throne supreme...

JOHN MILTON, *PARADISE LOST*, BOOK 5

left: **Satan plunges into the River Styx, illustration to *Paradise Lost*,
Richard Edmond Flatters, 1868, French**

At the end of John Milton's *Paradise Lost* Book 6, the archangel Raphael
described the final battle against Satan. The Son of God was sent in the
heavenly chariot, wheels within wheels and borne by cherubs, surrounded by
the army of the saints. Satan and his horde were driven to the crystal wall of
heaven, and through a breach into the "wasteful Deep." Milton had in mind here
the waste and void of Genesis 1, the chaotic state outside the light of heaven
which existed before the visible world was created. Here, Satan is shown falling
into the deep.

I saw there seven stars like great burning mountains ... And the angel said: "This place is the end of heaven and earth; it is the prison for the stars and the powers of heaven. And the stars which roll over on the fire are the ones who have broken the commandments of God..."

1 ENOCH 18

right: **Satan arousing the Rebel Angels, William Blake, 1808, English**
John Milton's *Paradise Lost* opens with the rebellion of the angels, which took place long before the creation of the visible world. Satan and his legions were driven from heaven to a place of chaos and darkness. Stunned at their expulsion, the fallen angels lay in a place of fire until aroused by Satan to counterattack and regain their place in heaven. Satan told his angels of something he had heard in heaven; there was to be a new world created, and a new type of creature. The council of fallen angels then decided not to try to recover heaven, but rather to explore the possibilities of working in the new creation. Satan set out to investigate. Here Blake depicts Satan addressing his angels as they lie in the place of fire and darkness, arousing them to action.

Angels and ministers of grace defend us!
Be thou a spirit of health, or goblin damn'd,
Bring with thee airs from heaven, or blasts
  from hell,
Be thy intents wicked, or charitable,
Thou com'st in such a questionable shape,
That I will speak to thee.

WILLIAM SHAKESPEARE, *HAMLET*, ACT **1**

left: **Lucifer, Prince of Hell, with devils around him, from Livre de la Vigne nostre Seigneur, c.1450–70, French**

Lucifer eventually became an arch-fiend, depicted here with seven heads. Good angels are always depicted in human form, but fallen and evil spirits frequently have grotesque form. In his vision, Daniel saw composite monsters—a lion's head with eagle's wings, a leopard with four wings. St. John saw the seven headed dragon, and then two monsters—one from the sea and one from the land. In the Dead Sea Scrolls, evil angels were terrifying dark creatures with snake-like faces. Demons were also thought to be like goats, possibly because "demon" and "goat" are the same word in Hebrew. Evil angels could even appear as angels of light when they wanted to deceive.

The Fractured Cosmos

Origen, the great Christian biblical scholar who died in 253 C.E., had a slightly different account of the fallen angels in his book *On First Principles*. No beings, he said, were created evil; their place in the hierarchy was the result of their own free choice. Ezekiel described a cherub who had walked in the Garden of Eden, among the sons of fire. The cherub had become proud and corrupted the divine knowledge, and so was driven from the holy place.[23] The cherub had not been created evil, but had freely chosen the iniquity that led to expulsion. Origen explained the story of Lucifer in the same way: "If, as some suppose, he was a being of darkness, why is he said to have been formerly called Lucifer, the light-bearer?" Jesus also spoke of Satan falling like lightning from heaven, so he must once have been there.[24]

Origen taught that any creature can repent and begin the upward progress, instructed by the angels and then by the higher powers, because any created being can change. "Differences of movement and will in either direction will lead to different states; angels may become men or daemons, and on the other hand daemons may become men or angels."[25] The ranks and roles of the angels were the result of their merits. They had all been created pure, serving God and keeping his laws of their own free will. The devil chose to oppose God, and the other powers, to a greater or lesser degree, followed him. Those who sinned a little remained as the ranks of angels, those who sinned greatly became the ranks of the daemons, and those who were between the two became human souls, constantly torn between the upward and downward movement. Those who fell away from unity with God were given charge of those who had fallen even further, and so forth throughout the hierarchy.[26]

Christ is risen from the dead
Trampling down death by death!
And on those in the tombs bestowing life!

PASCHAL TROPARION OF THE ORTHODOX CHURCH

previous page: **The Expulsion of the Devils from Arezzo (detail), from the fresco cycle of the The Life of St. Francis in the Upper Church of San Francesco in Assisi, Giotto di Bondone, 1297–99, Italian**

Driving out evil spirits, exorcism, has always been a part of Christian ministry. In Jesus's time, people believed that demons were the offspring of the fallen angels. When St. Francis visited the town of Arezzo in Italy, it was being destroyed by strife and discord, and he could see demons rejoicing at the trouble they had caused. He told Brother Sylvester to pray by the city gate and command the demons to leave. Peace returned to the city.

right: **The Harrowing of Hell, icon, Dionysius, late 15th century, Greek**

The resurrection of Christ was the final triumph over evil powers. Here, Christ rises from the dead on the broken doors of hell, releasing those who had been imprisoned by the fallen angels.

234

Interview with Philip Pullman

Award-winning children's author

How did you use the notion of angels in writing the trilogy
His Dark Materials?

To begin with, I was uneasy about the notion of using angels at all, until I realized that I could take a hint from Paradise Lost and view them not as actual beings but as analogues of states of mind. My other imagined beings, such as daemons, function in the same way. I imagine my angels as crystallizations of something called Dust, which is an embodiment of conscious knowledge and wisdom. One important way in which they differ from human beings is that they lack, and consequently envy, the vivid power of our physical senses.

In my cosmological scheme, the original war in heaven was just a rebellion against a tyrannical Authority. Inspired by the Sophia, or Wisdom, the rebel angels resolved to liberate the animal creatures who were evolving in every world as a result of the natural operations of matter, by bringing them the knowledge that would enable them to grow toward their true selves. This knowledge is symbolized by the Dust of the story, which is hated and feared by the Church and called by the name of Sin.

Like every human organisation, the Church has become an organisation that seeks only to perpetuate its own power. The struggle continues to this day. The liberating angels continue to work in secret, by inspiring great human teachers such as Jesus.

And What of the Spectres?

The Spectres of Indifference are a way of picturing the fatal nature of melancholy and accidie. They feed on Dust, and thus children, who have less of it, are immune, while adults succumb. The Spectres were let into the world by men of learning who were inquiring into the deepest nature of things, and thought that the bonds of creation could be negotiated.

Note from the author: This is remarkably like the image of the bonds of the cosmic covenant which can be broken through human sin. In the biblical picture it is wrath that enters through the breach. Wrath as indifference is an interesting point to ponder—Indifference destroying the creation.

NOTES

1 ROMANS 8. **2** REVELATION 12. **3** REVELATION 20. **4** ISAIAH 14. **5** ISAIAH 1. **6** MATTHEW 2.
7 1 ENOCH 8 & 69. **8** REVELATION 12. **9** 1 ENOCH 86. **10** 1 ENOCH 90. **11** JOB 1.
12 ZECHARIAH 3. **13** 1 CHRONICLES 21. **14** MATTHEW 4 & LUKE 4. **15** MARK 10. **16** LUKE 22.
17 REVELATION 12. **18** REVELATION 18. **19** REVELATION 20. **20** 2 CORINTHIANS 11. **21** LUKE 10.
22 HEBREWS 1. **23** REVELATION 12. **24** REVELATION 13. **25** SURAS 2, 7, 15, 17, 18, 20, 28.
26 REVELATION 12. **27** HEBREWS 7. **28** EZEKIEL 28. **29** OFP 1.5. **30** LUKE 10. **31** OFP 1.7.
32 OFP 1.8

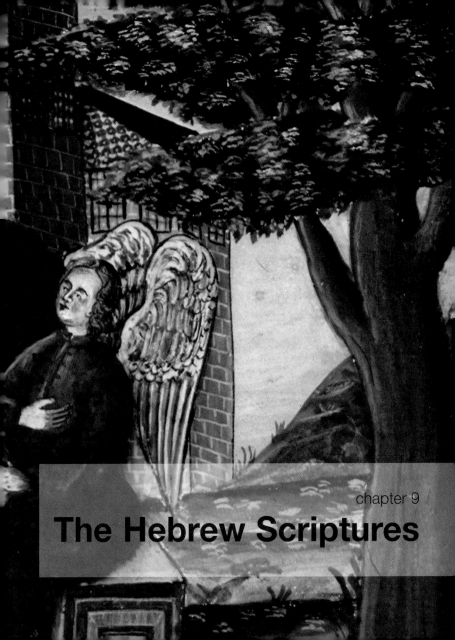

chapter 9

The Hebrew Scriptures

The Heavenly Hosts

We have learned from God the most excellent of our teachings and the most holy part of our law, by means of angels...

JOSEPHUS ANTIQUITIES 15.136

The most ancient title for the God of Israel was "the Lord of Hosts,"[1] the Lord of the angels. The Lord was enthroned and surrounded by the host of heaven;[2] the Lord came from Sinai with a host of holy ones,[3] and the sons of God in heaven challenged the Lord to test his servant Job.[4] The early Christian writers said that Judaism was a religion of angels, because the key events in Israel's history had involved angels, and the law of Moses was itself like a guardian angel to them. The manna in the wilderness had been the bread of angels, and their whole way of life had been revealed by angels, even the details of their temple and its sacred furnishings.[5] The angels did not only teach them; they also guarded those whom they had taught.

Sometimes the winds and weathers were described as angels. When David heard the sound of "marching" in the treetops, he knew that the Lord had gone ahead of him into battle,[6] and the Psalmist described the angels as winds—although the word here could also mean spirits.[7] In a great battle against the kings of Canaan, torrential rain made their iron chariots useless in the mud, and so poets sang of stars—angels—fighting for Israel, and the torrents of the River Kishon sweeping their enemy away.[8] The angels protected the faithful,[9] and destroyed their enemies.[10] When Jacob had run away, he saw angels on a ladder between heaven and earth, and knew that the Lord was still with him.[11] Angels could also bring judgment, as when the

Destroyer passed through Egypt on the night of the Exodus,[12] or when King David saw an angel with a drawn sword, about to bring plague on Jerusalem because of his sin.[13] Isaiah described the angels of peace weeping bitterly at the state of the land.[14]

When the stories were retold, there were far more angels than in the original text. Later tradition knew, for example, that there had been a fierce debate among the angels when God proposed to create Adam.[15] The original Adam had worn garments of light, not garments of skin;[16] he had been the glorious image of God,[17] eating the food of the angels in Eden, and the angels had to worship him.[18] He was the heavenly Man, the angel king of the earth who was endowed with divine Wisdom.[19] The angels taught Noah how to cure the diseases brought by the fallen angels.[20] The angels wept when Abraham prepared to sacrifice Isaac,[21] an angel led Rebecca to the well to meet Eliezer,[22] and when she first saw Isaac she saw his guardian angel.[23] The early Christians knew these extra angels: Stephen and Paul both said that the Law had been given on Sinai by angels,[24] and this is also what the Hebrew Christians believed.[25]

previous page: **The hospitality of Abraham (detail), from the Leipnik Passover Haggadah, Joseph Leipnik, 1740, North German**

Three men—angels—appeared to Abraham as he sat by his tent, near the great oak trees at Mamre. The storyteller says it was the Lord who visited Abraham, but it is not clear whether the Lord was accompanied by two other "men" or whether—as later tradition implied—the Lord was somehow all three of them. Abraham offered them bread, meat, and milk, and they ate the food. Angels do not usually eat, but these angels ate both meat and milk at the same meal, forbidden under later Jewish law. They came to tell Abraham that Sarah would have a son, and that Sodom would be destroyed.

Thou didst give thy people the food of angels, and without their toil, thou didst supply them from heaven with bread ready to eat...

WISDOM 16.20

right: **Gathering of Manna in the Desert, Giambattista Tiepolo, 1741, Italian**

During their forty years in the desert, the Israelites ate manna—meaning "what is it?"—which they gathered each morning. It looked like hoarfrost and tasted like honey, but did not keep fresh for more than a day, except over the Sabbath. They ground it and either baked bread or made a porridge. At the end of their wanderings, a jar of manna was placed in the sanctuary, to remind them of their time in the desert. Later writers said it was the grain of heaven, the bread of angels. Jesus contrasted himself with the manna, the bread of heaven which sustained only the body, and he promised the hidden manna to his faithful followers.

The angels on high took Isaac and brought him to the school house of Shem the Great and he was there for three years...
Satan went and told Sarah that Abraham had slaughtered Isaac. And Sarah arose and cried out and was choked and died of anguish.

TARGUM PS. JONATHAN TO GENESIS 22

left: **The Sacrifice of Isaac, Rembrandt, 1635, Dutch**

Abraham was tested by God many times, but the greatest was the command to sacrifice Isaac, his wife Sarah's only son. When everything was prepared, the angel of the Lord told Abraham to desist, and he offered instead a ram caught in a nearby thicket. The angel of the Lord called a second time and promised Abraham a reward for his obedience: his descendants would be numerous and a blessing to all the earth. The early Christians knew another version of this story, which is found in Jewish texts. Isaac was sacrificed and then raised from the dead. The Bible story does say that only Abraham returned to his waiting servants—Isaac is not mentioned.

Therefore as guardians are appointed for men who have to pass by an unsafe road, so an angel guardian is assigned to each man as long as he is a wayfarer. When, however, he arrives at the end of life, he no longer has an angel guardian; but in the Kingdom he will have an angel to reign with him, in hell a demon to punish him.

THOMAS AQUINAS, *SUMMA* 1.113

right: **Jacob's Ladder, School of Avignon, c. 1490, French**

When Jacob fled from his brother Esau, he traveled across the desert toward Haran, and spent the night at Bethel, where he had a stone for his pillow. In his dream he saw a ladder with angels on it, going up into heaven. The Lord stood beside him, and promised to be with him to bring him back safely, and to give the land to his descendants. Jacob realized he was in a holy place and declared: "This is none other than the house of God and this is the gate of heaven." Jesus alluded to this story when he said to Nathaniel that he too would see angels ascending and descending on the Son of Man.

Messengers

Angels in the Hebrew Scriptures are messengers, because human beings perceive them as messengers from God. This is what they do, not what they are. There are many other names for these heavenly beings, but much of the knowledge about angels has been lost, and so we no longer know exactly what these names mean. There were mighty ones, ministers and hosts,[26] sons of God,[27] watchers and holy ones,[28] cherubim and seraphim. We do not know, for example, what was meant by a "watcher" and how a watcher differed from a holy one. Some angels were described as gods *'elohim*,[29] a word that can also mean God. When Psalm 8 says that humans were made a little less than *'elohim*, does it mean they were almost angels, or almost God? This is clearly an important distinction.

Sometimes the word *mal'ak* in the Hebrew Scriptures means a messenger in the everyday sense, as when the king of Tyre sent messengers to King David with a consignment of cedar wood,[30] or Nehemiah sent messengers to Sanballat about rebuilding the wall of Jerusalem.[31] Sometimes, however, it could mean either a heavenly or an earthly messenger, and so when an unnamed "angel" spoke to a prophet, this could have been an ordinary person with a message from the Lord.[32] When Isaiah spoke of an embassy to Ethiopia, he said "Go, you swift/light messengers/angels to a people tall and smooth."[33] Was he thinking of angels or human diplomats? There is no way of knowing if Isaiah imagined angels or human messengers taking messages to Ethiopia.

The early Christians often called Jesus Christ "the Angel," because he was supremely a messenger from God, as John's Gospel makes clear. But the early Christians also emphasized that he was enthroned above the angels because he was the Son of God,[34] so he was far more than just an angel. The Hebrew scriptures describe the appearance of an angel in many ways. Job's friend had a terrifying experience: a whisper in a night vision, a spirit passing his face, and then an image before him whose details he could not see. There was silence and then a voice.[35] Often an angel was described simply as "a man," and we have no means of knowing if he was a heavenly or a human being. Joshua saw "a man" with a drawn sword, just before he attacked Jericho. This "man" said he was the captain of the Lord's host, so he must have been an angel.[36] When Daniel was praying, "the man" Gabriel flew to him, and we know Gabriel was an angel. Later he later saw a shining "man" dressed in linen.[37] The prophet Ezekiel saw "a man" of bronze who showed him the plan of the temple, and this "man", too, was an angel.[38]

following page: **Then the Lord answered Job out of the Whirlwind, William Blake, 1825, British**
Job had been questioning the justice of God. Why had he suffered? The Lord spoke to Job from the whirlwind and reminded him that he did not have the ancient wisdom of the angels of Day One. He had not witnessed the origin of all things, when the Morning Stars sang the creation into being and the sons of God celebrated. He did not even know about the visible world, the ways of the mountain goat and the ostrich. How could he hope to understand the ways of God?

Now a word was brought to me stealthily,
my ear received the whisper of it.
Amid thoughts from visions of the night,
When deep sleep falls on men,
Dread came upon me, and trembling,
Which made all my bones shake.
A spirit glided past my face;
The hair of my flesh stood up.
It stood still,
But I could not discern its appearance.
A form was before my eyes;
There was silence, then I heard a voice:
"Is a man more righteous than God
or more pure than his Creator?
Even in his angels he puts not trust,
And his angels he charges with error;
How much more those who dwell in houses of clay,
Whose foundation is in the dust,
Who are crushed before the moth.
Between morning and evening they are destroyed;
They perish for ever without any regarding it."

JOB 4

13

Who is this that darkeneth counsel by words without knowledge

Then the Lord answered Job out of the Whirlwind

Who maketh the Clouds his Chariot & walketh on the Wings of the Wind

the Drops of the Dew

Hath the Rain   a Father & who hath begotten

W Blake invenit & sculp

London Published as the Act directs March 8: 1825 by William Blake N 3 Fountain Court Strand

Proof

Neither Abraham nor Isaac nor Jacob nor any other man ever saw the Father and Lord of all things and of Christ himself, who is beyond words; but they saw him who is, according to his will, both God his Son and his Angel from doing his will and serving him.

ST. JUSTIN MARTYR, *DIALOGUE WITH TRYPHO 127*

left: **The angel appearing to Sarah, Giambattista Tiepolo, 1726–28, Italian**
Sarah, wife of Abraham, was childless, and too old to have a child. When the Lord visited them at Mamre, he told Abraham that Sarah would have a son, despite her age. Sarah was listening at the door, and when she laughed at the Lord's prediction, he rebuked her for not believing him. The identity of the three "men" in this story is not clear, but the one who spoke to Abraham and Sarah was the Lord, the scene depicted here. Sarah's only son was named Isaac, which means laughter.

right: The flight of Lot and his family from Sodom, Peter Paul Rubens, c. 1615, Flemish

Two of the three men—angels—who visited Abraham at Mamre went on to Sodom. They were almost raped by the men of the city, but were rescued by Abraham's nephew, Lot. The angels warned him that the city was soon to be destroyed because of the evil ways of its people, and they told him to take his wife and two daughters from the city. After they had left, the cities of Sodom and Gomorrah were destroyed.

And in those days Noah saw the earth, that it had sunk down and its destruction was nigh... And he cried aloud to his grandfather Enoch... And Enoch said, "A command has gone forth from the presence of the Lord concerning those that dwell on the earth, that their ruin is accomplished because they have learned all the secrets of the angels and all the violence of the satans and all their powers...

1 ENOCH 65

left: **God orders Noah to build the Ark, Marcantonio Raimondi, 16th century, Italian**

When the earth had been corrupted by the fallen angels, God warned Noah that the earth would be destroyed. He told him to build the ark, so that his family and some of every living creature would be saved. Here Noah's three sons—Shem, Ham, and Japhet—are small boys, but by the time the ark was finished they had wives. God is depicted as an angel figure, with three small boys clustered about him to indicate the Three in One of Christian belief. The Hebrew storyteller imagined the Lord in human form; he came to earth to shut Noah safely into the ark.

The angel of the Lord found Hagar by a spring of water in the wilderness, the spring on the way to Shur. And he said, "Hagar, maid of Sarai, where have you come from and where are you going?" She said, "I am fleeing from my mistress Sarai." The angel of the Lord said to her, "Return to your mistress and submit to her." The angel of the Lord also said to her, "I will so greatly multiply your descendants that they cannot be numbered for multitude."

GENESIS 16

left: **The Angel appears to Hagar in the Desert, Ferdinand Bol, 17th century, Dutch**

When Abraham's wife Sarah was childless, he took her maid Hagar as a concubine, but domestic strife ensued. Sarah drove Hagar away into the desert where the angel of the Lord met her. Here, in a scene reminiscent of the Annunciation, the angel tells Hagar to return to her mistress. She is pregnant and her son is to be named Ishmael. Ishmael became the father of twelve sons, who were the ancestors of the Arabs.

Then the Lord opened the eyes of Balaam, and he saw the angel of the Lord standing in the way, with his drawn sword in his hand; and he bowed his head and fell on his face.

NUMBERS 22

right: **Balaam and his Ass, James J. Tissot, 1886–94, French**

Balaam was a diviner, hired by the princes of Moab and Midian to curse the advancing Israelites and halt them. He set out on his ass, with the princes of Moab and two servants, but his way was barred by the angel of the Lord, standing with a drawn sword. Only his ass saw the angel, and she turned aside and refused to continue. Balaam, threatened her and she protested to him. Then Balaam also saw the angel, and instead of cursing Israel, he blessed them three times. Some early Christians referred enigmatically to a "Balaam" in their own time. This may have been St. Paul, immediately after his conversion, when few trusted him. He too was employed to persecute the Israelites, but was stopped on his way by the Lord.

The golden moments in the stream of life rush past us and we see nothing but sand; the angels come to visit us, and we only know them when they are gone.

GEORGE ELIOT

left: **Gideon's Sacrifice (detail), Francesco Fontebasso, 18th century, Italian**
The angel of the Lord appeared under the great oak tree at Ophrah, and called Gideon to free his people from the terror of the Midianites. Gideon asked the angel to accept a food offering, and was told to set meat and unleavened bread on a rock, and pour over them some broth. The angel did not eat the food; he touched it with the tip of his staff and it was consumed with fire. The angel vanished. An altar was built where the angel of the Lord appeared. This was the custom in Israel, before Jerusalem was established as the only place of worship. Wherever the Lord appeared, an altar was set up to mark the site.

King Nebuchadnezzar was astonished and rose up in haste. He said to his counsellors, "Did we not cast three men bound into the fire?" They answered the king, "True, O king." He answered, "But I see four men loose, walking in the midst of the fire, and they are not hurt; and the appearance of the fourth is like a son of the gods."

DANIEL 3

right: **Shadrach, Meshach, and Abednego in the Fiery Furnace, Simeon Solomon, late 19th century, British**

Daniel tells the story of the young men whom Nebuchadnezzar, king of Babylon, threw into a furnace. A fourth figure appeared, an angel of God sent to protect his servants.

The Angel of the Lord

Most of the well-known angel stories in the Hebrew Scriptures concern "the angel of the Lord," which probably does not mean "an angel sent by the Lord," but rather an appearance of the Lord himself, a theophany. Before Samson was born, his parents had visions: the angel of the Lord appeared to his mother and she described him as "a man of the *'elohim*" whose appearance was like an angel of the *'elohim*. The pair eventually realized that the heavenly being, who refused to reveal his name, was the angel of the Lord. When they offered a sacrifice to the Lord, the angel went up to heaven in the flames.[39] This could have been an appearance of the Lord, but the account is ambiguous. The story of Gideon is similar: the Lord and the angel of the Lord appear as two names for the same figure.[40]

The same is true in Zechariah's vision of heaven, when he saw Joshua being given his vestments to serve as the high priest.[41] The figure presiding in this scene has three names: the Lord, the angel of the Lord, and the Angel.

Isaiah gives the best examples of the various names for the Lord. Describing the Exodus from Egypt when the Lord saved the Israelites from slavery, he wrote "the angel of his presence saved them."[42] When the Greek version of Isaiah was made about 250 B.C.E., some people must have been thinking that the angel of his Presence was another angel, and so the translation made it absolutely clear that this was not so. The line became: "Not an elder nor an angel but he Himself saved them." The angel of the presence was the Lord.

Elsewhere Isaiah often called the Lord "the Holy One of Israel," and the Holy One simply means "the angel."[43] He also recorded the most spectacular of all the stories about the angel of the Lord. When Jerusalem was threatened by the Assyrians in 701 B.C.E., the angel of the Lord destroyed their army before it could attack the city.[44]

People who wore the Name of the Lord were also thought to be the angel of the Lord. We know that the high priest was venerated as the angel of the Lord, since he wore the Name on his forehead, and when he came into the temple court, people knelt before him. On Palm Sunday, when the crowd accompanying Jesus into Jerusalem cried out "Blessed is he who comes in/with the Name of the Lord,"[45] they were proclaiming Jesus as the angel of the presence, the Lord himself. This was an ancient belief: whoever led the Israelites on their journey from Mount Sinai was said to have the Name of the Lord "within him." Nobody knows what this means, but the person was described as an angel.[46]

The prophets also were described as angels, because they were messengers of God.[47] The prophets began their oracles: "Thus says the Lord…," because they believed that they spoke from the Lord and as the Lord.[48] They were his angels. The name of the prophet Malachi simply means "My angel," and it may not have been his name at all, but a description of his role. The Greek version of the book begins: "A record of the word of the Lord to Israel by the hand of his angel." "Malachi" said that a priest was an "angel" of the Lord.[49] Zechariah said an angel spoke "in him," translating the Hebrew literally,[50] just as King David had claimed that the Spirit of the Lord had spoken *in* him.[51]

Even in the oldest stories, the Lord and the angel of the Lord are described in human form. The early chapters of Genesis imply that the Lord came to earth and had human characteristics: the Lord shut Noah into the ark;[52] the Lord enjoyed the smell of Noah's sacrifice;[53] the Lord came down to see the tower being built in Babel.[54] The Lord appeared to Abraham at Mamre, ate a meal and went on his way.[55] When Abraham was about to sacrifice Isaac, the angel of the Lord called to him, and told him not to kill the boy: "For I now know that you fear God, seeing that you have not withheld your son from *me*."[56] The angel of the Lord appeared to Moses in the burning bush and the Lord spoke to him.[57] The angel of the Lord stopped Balaam, but at first only his ass saw the figure with a drawn sword standing in their path.[58] The angel of the Lord brought the people out of Egypt;[59] the angel of the Lord led the heavenly armies against the kings of Canaan.[60]

The first Christians said that these accounts of the Lord or the angel of the Lord were pre-incarnation appearances of Jesus. "No one has ever seen God," (meaning God the Father) wrote St. John,[61] and so all the appearances in the Old Testament must have been the Son. Abraham had known him,[62] and Isaiah in the temple had seen the Son enthroned.[63] In the Greek translation of the Hebrew Scriptures, made long before the time of Jesus, Isaiah's four names for the Messiah— Wonderful Counselor, Mighty God, Everlasting Father, Prince of Peace—became simply the Angel of Great Counsel.[64] Since much of the early Church used the Greek Old Testament, this was how they would have understood the Messiah, and "Angel" was a title used for the Messiah until the fourth century C.E.

right: **Moses on Mount Sinai (detail), Sistine Chapel walls, Vatican, Rome, Cosimo Rosselli, 1481–82, Italian**
In the time of Jesus, the Jews believed that the Law had been given to them on Sinai by angels, but the Hebrew Scriptures describe only the cloud that settled on Mount Sinai and the Glory of the Lord like a devouring fire on the top of the mountain.

Interview with Professor Alan F. Segal

Professor of Jewish Studies, Barnard College,
Columbia University, New York

What is the role of the Angels in Judaism today?

Judaism acknowledges angels, but much depends on local custom and ceremonies. Angels are in the Bible and are important in the Hellensitic period, but they are not in the Mishnah, the first great piece of rabbinic literature. Angels are in rabbinic Jewish tradition, but there are limits on the interaction and intermediation of angels, which Jews do not normally surpass.

A Jewish child today will encounter angels in synagogue liturgy, with the frequent use of the Kidusha, the Holy Holy Holy of Isaiah 6, and Jews welcome the Sabbath as a heavenly bride with her angelic accompaniment. Jews worldwide sing, Shalom Aleichem, asking for the blessing of peace from the angels of peace and saying that these angels come directly from the King, the King of Kings, the Holy One, Blessed Be He. That the angels are directly under the control of God is crucial for understanding the limitations of contemporary Jewish traditions about angels.

Midrash, and occasionally Talmud, names individual angels, but the synagogue service does not, mentioning only classes of angels: Ministering angels, Seraphim, Angels of Peace. Ordinary rabbinic Judaism today—Orthodox, Conservative, or Reform—is unwilling to name specific angels or address prayers to them. All petitionary prayers are addressed to God or to God's angels in general. This clearly establishes a border—perhaps because the rabbis were unhappy with Christ devotion, where Jesus is called LORD and worshipped as divine.

Many angels are named in midrash: Sammael—Satan as part of God's retinue, Metatron—the angel who carries God's name, and the

Angel of Death. The archangels—Raphael, Uriel, Michael, Gabriel, and many more—are discussed, and midrashic characters talk to them, but no one as a rule prays to them. Elijah frequently reports what happened in heaven when God took decisions, but he does not intercede nor receive devotion in the Christian sense.

An exception might be the magical, mystical, and theurgic literature—not mainstream rabbinic Judaism, but various communities have their own customs. Sefer Raziel (the book of Raziel) keeps a house safe from fire, and magical bowls hold petitionary prayers to angels and exorcisms of demons. The Hekhalot literature has spells involving angels, and Sefer Ha-razim (the book of Mysteries) a Hebrew book of uncertain origin, has angelic names and spells for controlling them. Hasidic rabbis are often described as semi-divine in life and as saints when they die, and the hasidim do address prayers to them. North African Jews venerate saints just as Muslims there venerate Marabouts, but on the whole Jewish tradition avoids the intermediation of angels or saints.

NOTES

1 ISAIAH 6. **2** 1 KINGS 22. **3** DEUTERONOMY 33 AND PSALM 68. **4** JOB 1 **5** WISDOM 16.
6 2 SAMUEL 5. **7** PSALM 104. **8** JUDGES 5. **9** PSALMS 34 AND 91. **10** PSALM 78.49. **11** GENESIS
28. **12** EXODUS12. **13** 2 SAMUEL 24. **14** ISAIAH 33. **15** GENESIS RABBAH VIII. **16** GENESIS
RABBAH XX. **17** 3 BARUCH 4. **18** LIFE OF ADAM AND EVE 4 AND 13. **19** 2 ENOCH 30.
20 JUBILEES 10. **21** GENESIS RABBAH LXV. **22** GENESIS RABBAH LIX. **23** GENESIS RABBAH LX.
24 ACTS 7.53; GALATIANS 3.19. **25** HEBREWS 2.2 **26** PSALMS 103. **27** JOB 1 AND 38. **28** DANIEL
4. **29** PSALM 82. **30** 1 CHRONICLES 14. **31** NEHEMIAH 6. **32** 1 KINGS 13.18. **33** ISAIAH 18.
34 HEBREWS 1. **35** JOB 4. **36** JOSHUA 5. **37** DANIEL 9 & 10. **38** EZEKIEL 40. **39** JUDGES 13.
40 JUDGES 6. **41** ZECHARIAH 3. **42** ISAIAH 63. **43** ISAIAH 1. **44** ISAIAH 37. **45** PSALM 118 &
MARK 11. **46** EXODUS 23.20-23. **47** 2 CHRONICLES 36.16. **48** AMOS 1 **49** MALACHI 2.
50 ZECHARIAH 1.9.13.14. **51** 2 SAMUEL 23. **52** GENESIS 7.16. **53** GENESIS 8.21. **54** GENESIS
11.5. **55** GENESIS 18. **56** GENESIS 22. **57** EXODUS 3. **58** NUMBERS 22. **59** JUDGES 2.
60 JUDGES 5. **61** JOHN 1. **62** JOHN 8. **63** JOHN 12. **64** ISAIAH 9.

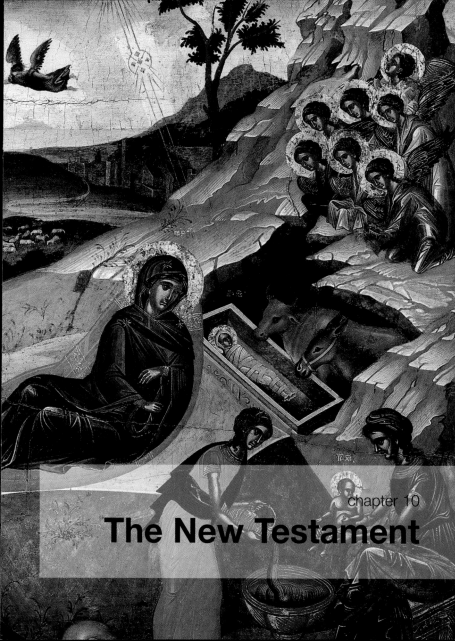

chapter 10

The New Testament

Angels in the Life of Jesus

The first Christians lived among angels. They wove angels into the story of Jesus, they described themselves as angels and lived an angel lifestyle, they worshiped with angels, and felt the presence of angels among them. Their prophets had visions of angels, and they expected Jesus to come from heaven with his host of fiery angels. Jesus himself, however, was enthroned above the angels.

Angels mark the beginning and end of Jesus' earthly life. At the point where he comes from heaven—the Nativity—and at the point where he returns to heaven—the Resurrection and Ascension—there are angels. Elsewhere Jesus spoke of angels serving him when he was tempted by Satan in the desert,[1] and of an angel strengthening him when he prayed in Gethsemane.[2] Since Jesus was alone at these times, he himself must have spoken about the angels. People believed that an angel moved the waters of the pool at Bethsaida,[3] and some said they heard the voice of an angel speaking to Jesus.[4]

Angels appear in the story of Jesus' birth. Gabriel appeared in the temple to tell Zechariah he would be the father of John the Baptist,[5] and then he told Mary she would be the mother of the Son of God.[6] An angel of the Lord told Joseph in a dream that Mary had conceived by the Holy Spirit and the child should be named Jesus.[7] An angel of the Lord told the shepherds that the Messiah had been born in Bethlehem, and a heavenly host appeared, praising God.[8] An angel of

previous page: Icon of the Nativity, c. 1480–1500, Creto-Venetian Greek
In any icon of the Nativity, heaven and earth are joined. Here, the Glory lights up the night sky, angels wing their way to tell the shepherds and the heavenly host hovers over the crib. To the left, St. Joseph sits perplexed as Satan, disguised as a shepherd, tempts him to believe that the birth was not a miracle.

the Lord told Joseph in another dream to take Mary and her child to Egypt, to escape the wrath of King Herod.[9]

Angels appear in the Easter story, sometimes described as "men in white." Mark says the three women saw a young man in white inside the empty tomb,[10] Matthew says they saw an angel roll the stone from the entrance to the tomb.[11] Luke and John say there were two angels or two men in white.[12] When Jesus was parted from his disciples and taken to heaven in a cloud, two men in white told them he would return from heaven in the same way.[13]

When the early Christians expounded the Nativity stories they explained the role of the angels. Some said that the shepherds at Bethlehem were in fact the shepherd angels, the guardian angels in charge of the nations who had been losing their battle against evil and had almost given up. When his own people were being overwhelmed by evil, the Lord came into the world to help the shepherd angels in their struggle. The heavenly host who appeared to the shepherds bringing the good news were the angels attending the Lord as he came to earth to begin his battle against evil.

The Resurrection and Ascension marked the return of the Lord to his place in heaven, when angels bore him up in triumph, singing Psalm 24: "Lift up your heads, O gates, and be lifted up, O ancient doors, that the King of Glory may come in." The angels were astonished that the incarnate Lord was exalted to the highest place in heaven, and that human nature, which had been driven from Paradise, was now enthroned in heaven.

This way of understanding the role of the angels in the life of Jesus must have been part of early Christianity, even though it is not obvious in the New Testament. Their role in the Incarnation and Ascension is described, for example, in the Ascension of Isaiah, which was compiled at the end of the first century C.E. Someone writing as

Isaiah had a vision of God Most High sending the Lord down through the seven heavens and into the world. This was the realm of Satan and his angels, described here as the prince of this world and the angels of the air. (Paul also knew Satan by this name—the prince of the power of the air who worked through the sons of disobedience.)[14] Since the Lord's true identity was hidden, Satan incited the rulers in Jerusalem, and they crucified him. Then the Lord ascended again through the seven heavens, receiving the homage of the angels as he passed. He was enthroned on the right of the Great Glory, with the Angel of the Holy Spirit enthroned on the left. There are other early Christian writings with a similar description of the Incarnation and Ascension.

right: **The Vision of Zacharias, James J. Tissot, 1886–94, French**
St. Luke begins the story of the Nativity by describing the priest Zechariah's vision in the temple in Jerusalem. While he was making the incense offering, Gabriel appeared by the incense altar and told him that his wife Elisabeth would have a son, John the Baptist. There are other records of priests receiving visions in the temple. In about 160 B.C.E., when the Jews were fighting for their independence, Onias the high priest had a vision of Jeremiah giving him a golden sword to defend his people.

The angel Gabriel to Mary came
His wings as drifted snow, his eyes of
  flame;
"All Hail" said he, "thou lowly maiden Mary.
Most highly favored Lady."
Gloria.

"BASQUE CAROL" ADAPTED BY S. BARING GOULD

left: **The Annunciation, with St. Luke the Evangelist, Benedetto Bonfigli, 1455–60, Italian**

St. Luke is the only Gospel writer to describe the Annunciation, when the Archangel Gabriel came to Mary and told her she would be the Mother of the Son of God. Here, Luke is writing his gospel as Gabriel, with his symbol the lily, appears to Mary. God the Father, surrounded by the angels of his Glory, sends the Holy Spirit in the form of a dove. Traditionally, Mary received the Spirit through her ear, as shown here, because she heard the word and accepted it.

As Joseph was a-walking
He heard an Angel sing:
"This night shall be born
Our Heav'nly King.

He neither shall be born
In housen nor in hall,
Nor in the place of Paradise,
But in an ox's stall."

ANONYMOUS, FROM "AS JOSEPH WAS A-WALKING,"
TRADITIONAL FRENCH CAROL

right: **The Dream of Saint Joseph, Francesco Goya, 1771, Spanish**
Matthew describes St. Joseph's experience of the Nativity, and how he was
troubled by Mary's unexplained pregnancy. Here, as so often happens, an angel
speaks to Joseph in his dream, and tells him that Mary is carrying the divine
child who is to be named Jesus. This fulfilled the prophecy in Isaiah, that the
Virgin would bear a Son.

And in that region there were shepherds out in the field, keeping watch over their flock by night. And an angel of the Lord appeared to them, and the glory of the Lord shone around them, and they were filled with fear. And the angel said to them, "Be not afraid; for behold, I bring you good news of great joy which will come to all people. For to you is born this day in the city of David a Savior, who is Christ the Lord. And this will be a sign for you: You will find a babe wrapped in swaddling cloths and lying in a manger." And suddenly there was with the angel a multitude of the heavenly host praising God and saying, "Glory to God in the highest, and on earth, peace, good will among men."

LUKE 2.8–14

left: **The Angels Appearing to the Shepherds, William Blake, 1809, British**
Luke's account of the birth of Jesus makes clear that it was an event both in heaven and on earth. The first Christians said that when the heavenly Lord came to earth, he was attended by his angels, the glorious host who appeared to the shepherds of Bethlehem. Here Blake captures well the sense of the unity of the angels.

Angels and archangels
May have gathered there,
Cherubim and seraphim
Thronged the air,
But only His mother
In her maiden bliss
Worshipped the Beloved
With a kiss.

CHRISTINA GEORGINA ROSSETTI, "A CHRISTMAS CAROL"

right: **The Nativity (detail), Agnolo Gaddi, 1392–95, Italian**

Heaven and earth rejoice at the Nativity. Isaiah 9 described angels celebrating
the birth of their new son who would sit on the throne of David. Here, the angels
proclaim the same news to the shepherds, that the Savior has been born in the
city of David, and the host gathers around the Child. There was a prophecy in
Isaiah 1 that the ox and the ass would recognize their master, but Israel would
not, and so the animals here remind us that many did not understand the
mystery of the Nativity.

In those days Jesus came from Nazareth in Galilee and was baptized by John in the Jordan. And when he came up out of the water, immediately he saw the heavens opened and the Spirit descending upon him like a dove; and a voice came from heaven, "Thou art my beloved Son; with thee I am well pleased."

MARK 1

left: **The Baptism of Christ, Adam Elsheimer, 1598–1600, German**
The Gospels say that at his baptism, Jesus saw the heavens open and the Spirit come down on him. The early Christians understood this to be a vision of the heavenly throne chariot with the mighty angels. By the late sixteenth century however, angels were becoming playful little cherubs, very different from the original import of the vision. Here, Jesus is not even looking toward the opening heavens.

following page: **The Agony in the Garden, El Greco, 1590–95, Greek**
The earliest versions of St. Luke's Gospel describe the angel who appeared to Jesus in the garden, on the night he was betrayed and arrested. He prayed that the cup of suffering might be taken from him. While he was praying, his disciples fell asleep. Here, he accepts the cup from the angel, and so accepts his death.

left: The Crucifixion, from the fresco cycle of the Life of Christ, in the Arena Chapel, Padua, Giotto di Bondone, 1304–06, Italian
The death of Jesus was a cosmic event. Heaven and earth were mourning, shown here by the sorrowing angels above and the grieving disciples at the foot of the cross. Matthew, Mark, and Luke record darkness from noon until three o'clock, as Jesus hung dying on the cross.

Dead Christ supported by an Angel, Jacques de Backer, 17th century, Dutch

Just as the Jewish storytellers added angels to their tales in places where no angel is mentioned in the Bible, so too Christian artists felt free to add angels to their depiction of great events. Here, an angel supports Jesus after his death. There are many pictures of Mary holding the body of her Son, even though this is not described in the New Testament. The New Testament says only that Joseph of Arimathea and Nicodemus had the body taken down and buried, and that the women watched to see where he was entombed.

following page: **Why Seek Ye the Living among the Dead? John Rodham Spencer Stanhope, late 19th century, British**

The title of the picture is taken from Luke's account of Easter morning. St. Mark described how Mary Magdalene, Mary the mother of James, and Salome brought spice to Jesus' tomb on Easter morning, because there had not been time to bury him properly on Good Friday. They saw a young man dressed in white who told them that Jesus had risen from the dead and was no longer there. St. Matthew says they saw an angel, but a "man in white" is the usual way to describe an angel.

Now in the night whereon the Lord's day dawned, as the soldiers were keeping guard ... there came a great sound in the heaven, and they saw the heavens opened and two men descend thence, having a great light, and drawing near unto the sepulchre. And that stone which had been set on the door rolled away of itself ... and the sepulchre was opened and both of the young men entered in. When therefore those soldiers saw that, they waked up the centurion and the elders ... and while they were yet telling them the things which they had seen, they saw again three men come out of the sepulchre, and two of them sustaining the one, and a cross following after them. And of the two, they saw that their heads reached unto heaven, but of him that was led by them, that it overpassed the heavens. And they heard a voice out of the heavens saying: Hast thou preached to them that sleep? And an answer was heard from the cross saying: Yea.

GOSPEL OF PETER 9

left: **The Resurrection: The Angel Rolling the Stone away from the Sepulchre, William Blake, 1808, British**
Depicting resurrection from within the tomb is unusual, and here Blake captures the moment just before the events described in the New Testament. A mighty angel rolled away the stone and Mary Magdalene saw two angels in the tomb, one at the head and one at the feet of where Jesus had been lying. The linen grave clothes were all that remained.

Christ the Lord is risen today
Sons of men and angels say
"Alleluia."
Raise your joys and triumphs high
Sing ye heavens; thou earth reply
"Alleluia."

CHARLES WESLEY

right: **The Ascension of Christ, Perugino, late 15th century, Italian**
Christ surrounded by the bodiless powers—the cloud of Glory—ascends to
heaven, where the music of the angels will welcome him. Two angels look down
and speak to Mary and the disciples, saying that the Lord will return from
heaven in the same way.

Angels in the Earliest Church

For to what angel did God ever say, "Thou art my son, today I have begotten thee?"
Or again,
"I will be to him a father and he shall be to me a son"?
And again, when he brings the firstborn into the world he says,
"Let all God's angels worship him."

HEBREWS 1

The first Christians lived close to the angels: Peter and the apostles were released from prison by an angel of the Lord,[15] an angel sent Philip to meet the Ethiopian diplomat,[16] an angel told the Roman centurion Cornelius to send for Peter.[17] Paul had a dream vision of a man from Macedonia, asking him for help; he must have been the angel of Macedonia.[18] During the storm that eventually wrecked him on Malta, an angel appeared to Paul and told him he would reach Rome.[19]

Jesus had been enthroned above the angels,[20] and all ranks in heaven and earth worshiped him.[21] The first Christians lived with the hope that Jesus would soon return, appearing with his host of mighty angels to bring the Day of Judgment when sinners would be punished.[22] These angels were also called his *saints*, a word which means, literally, "holy ones."[23] The Christians also described themselves as "saints" and they believed they would join with the angels to bring judgement on the world.[24]

The Christians thought of themselves as angels on earth. Jesus had taught that angels were sons of God, living the life of heaven.[25] This heavenly life was called the resurrected life, and the Christians, who called themselves the children of God believed that they, too, were already resurrected and living as angels on earth. They had already been ressurected with Christ to the life of heaven and had left behind the ways of this world.[26] They could no longer have materialistic values. When they emerged from the water of baptism, they put on white clothes to symbolize their birth as angels.

Paul explained that resurrection meant returning to Adam's original state. Before he was expelled from Eden, he had been a heavenly being, not a mortal with a body that would perish.[27] Christians were heirs to the heritage of the angels,[28] and they would share the angel knowledge, understanding the heavenly love which it was impossible for human minds to comprehend.[29] They would receive revelation that even the angels had longed for,[30] although Peter does not tell us what this was. Perhaps it was seeing the Glory of God.

Paul began his letters to the churches with greetings to the saints, the angels, in Rome, Corinth, or Philippi. When he explained the Christian lifestyle it was the angel lifestyle. They were children of light, and should have no contact with the ways of darkness—immorality, impurity, levity.[31] They were the new generation of sons of God, replacing the fallen sons of God, the evil angels who had corrupted the creation. Christ was the Firstborn Son of God, said Paul, but the first of many.[32] The Christians looked forward to joining the host of angels in the city of God, which they called the heavenly Jerusalem.[33] This is described at the end of the Book of Revelation as the city with angels standing at its gates.

Stone walls do not a prison make,
  nor iron bars a cage.
Minds innocent and quiet take
  that for a hermitage:
If I have freedom in my love,
  and in my Soul am free,
Angels alone, that soar above,
  enjoy such liberty.

RICHARD LOVELACE, "TO ALTHEA FROM PRISON"

right: **The Liberation of St. Peter, Noël Hallé, 1764, French**

In the Acts of the Apostles there are several stories of miraculous release from prison. Peter and several apostles were released by an angel. Paul and Silas were released by a miraculous earthquake. Here Peter is released by an angel of the Lord. He had been sleeping between two soldiers when a light shone in the prison and Peter was led out through the iron gate which opened of its own accord.

The Book of Revelation

The Book of Revelation, the New Testament's most mysterious writing, is set in the angel world of the first Christians. The bishops were seen as the guardian angels of the seven churches in Asia Minor, just as the priests in the Jerusalem temple had called themselves angels, and the prophet John received heavenly letters for each of them.[34]

He was taken in a vision to stand before the heavenly throne, where he saw the four living creatures and the elders, and the Lamb enthroned. In the world of the angels, heavenly beings were described as "men" and human beings as animals, and so the Lamb enthroned was a vision of a human being set above the highest ranks of heaven. This was Adam restored to his original state. Once he was enthroned, the judgment began: the six seals of the scroll of judgment were opened, but four angels at the four corners of the earth withheld the final devastation until the servants of God had been saved.[35]

As the seventh seal was opened, seven angels with trumpets announced the descent of the Mighty Angel. After the sixth trumpet, he came from heaven wreathed in a rainbow and wrapped in a cloud and he gave new teaching to John his prophet. With the seventh and last trumpet, the Kingdom of heaven was established on earth.[36]

In his vision John saw an angel in heaven—"the woman clothed with the sun"—and she gave birth to a boy. A great red dragon, whose tail had swept one third of the stars down to earth—one third of the angels—was waiting to devour the child. He escaped and was taken up to the throne of God. Then there was war in heaven. St. Michael and his angels fought the dragon and his angels, and the dragon was forced down onto the earth, where he began to fight against the woman's other children.[37]

John then saw a beast coming out of the sea to fight against the saints/angels on earth, and the heavenly army about to come to their aid. Angels flew from heaven to announce that the Day of Judgment was at hand, and then angels came from the temple to call for the harvest of the earth. Angel reapers gathered the corn—representing good people—and then other angels gathered the grapes of wrath—representing evil people—and blood flowed from the winepress.[38]

Seven angel high priests came out from the holy of holies, carrying bowls of wrath, which they poured on the earth and on "Babylon," the wicked city. One of the angels showed John the great harlot, and explained that she was the wicked city. More angels came from heaven; one to announce the fall of the city, another to throw a great millstone into the sea as a sign that "Babylon" was destroyed.[39]

The host in heaven rejoiced at the fall of the city, and John heard them singing "Hallelujah," "Praise the Lord." The Lord then rode out from heaven with his angel army, all dressed in white linen and riding white horses, and an angel bound Satan for a thousand years in the bottomless pit. Then the saints began to reign on earth.[40]

In the final scenes of John's vision, one of the seven angels showed him the heavenly city, with twelve angels set at its twelve gates. The angel guide measured the city, which was built of gold and precious stones. Its gates stood open, but only the pure could enter. This was the city of angels, whose light was the Glory of God and the Lamb. The river of the Water of Life flowed through the city and watered the Tree of Life whose leaves would heal the nations. Those within the city had access to the Tree from which Adam and Eve had been barred through their disobedience. The disaster of Genesis had been reversed, and human beings were restored to their original angel state. All were angel high priests, bearing on their foreheads the Name, standing in the presence of God, and worshiping.[41]

left: **St. Michael Fighting the Dragon, Albrecht Dürer, 1498, German**

St. John saw the Archangel Michael and his angels fighting against the Devil and Satan, described as a red dragon with seven heads and ten horns. The evil powers were thrown down to earth, where they began to attack the children of the woman clothed with the sun. Jesus himself saw this vision: "I saw Satan fall like lightning from heaven," he said, and he gave his followers the power to tread on such snakes and scorpions.

following page: **The harvest is the end of the world and the reapers are angels, Roger Wagner, 1989, British**

The angel reapers are a positive image in the New Testament, symbolizing the gathering of the righteous before the Day of Judgment. John the Baptist prophesied one who would gather his wheat into the barn but burn the chaff. Jesus spoke about the angel reapers gathering the wheat into the barn, but burning the weeds. He saw the fields already white for harvest. St. John saw the Son of Man, crowned and seated on a cloud, coming forth to reap the harvest of the earth, to gather his own before the grapes of wrath were gathered and trampled. Here, the angel reapers work ahead of the imminent storm.

For the Lord himself will descend from heaven with a cry of command, with the archangel's call, and with a sound of the trumpet of God.

1 THESSALONIANS 4

right: **The woes of the second trumpet, from the Beatus of Liébana (The Escorial Beatus), 10th century, Spanish**

St. John saw seven angels standing before the heavenly throne. As each angel sounded his trumpet, one woe fell upon the earth. Here, with the second trumpet, a mountain burning with fire is thrown into the sea, one third of the sea becomes blood, a third of the living creatures die in the sea, and a third of the ships were destroyed. The trumpet was a signal for holy war. Since a mountain was the symbol of a great ruler, the burning mountain which here falls into the sea was probably Mark Antony, the Roman ruler defeated at the naval battle of Actium in 31 B.C.E. The sea was turned to blood, the ships were destroyed, and the living creatures—his men—died in the sea.

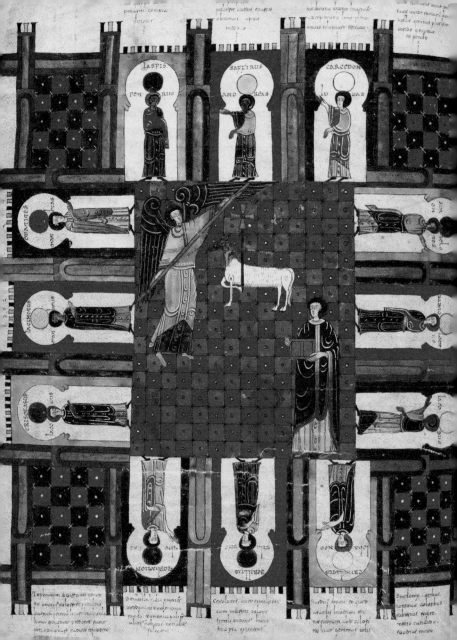

Then came one of the seven angels who had the seven bowls full of the seven last plagues, and spoke to me, saying, "Come, I will show you the bride, the wife of the Lamb." And in the Spirit he carried me away to a great high mountain, and showed me the holy city Jerusalem coming down out of heaven from God, having the Glory of God, its radiance like a most rare jewel, like a jasper, clear as crystal. It had a great high wall with twelve gates, and at the gates, twelve angels...

REVELATION 21

left: **New Jerusalem, from the Beatus of Liébana (The Facundus Beatus), 1047, Spanish**

When St. John saw the heavenly Jerusalem, there was an angel at each of the twelve gates. Another angel with a golden measuring rod showed St. John the city, and here he is recording the vision. At the center is the Lamb. In the tradition of the angels, heavenly figures are depicted as humans and mortals as animals. Here, a human being, the Lamb, has been taken into the highest heaven.

Interview with Professor Richard Bauckham
University of St. Andrews, Scotland

Are the angels a significant part of New Testament scholarship today? And does the current emphasis reflect accurately the world of the first Christians?

I guess you won't find many New Testament scholars writing books and articles about angels as such, though there are some. But there has been ongoing discussion about specific topics. For example, Paul's letters quite often refer to cosmic powers known by such terms as "powers," "rulers," "thrones," and "authorities." It is not always clear whether these are good or evil powers. Walter Wink [Professor of Biblical Interpretation, Auburn Seminary, New York City] sees these as the inner spiritual aspect of political and economic forces, a proposal that makes them more obviously relevant to a contemporary worldview. Angels have also featured in New Testament Christology, since some scholars argue that Christ is portrayed as an angel or like an angel, and it is certainly important to New Testament writers to insist on his superiority to the angels.

In general I think it is clear that angels were an unquestioned part of the worldview of the early Christians, but mostly there is no great interest in them for their own sake. Only two angels in the New Testament have names (Michael and Gabriel), in contrast with some Jewish literature. Mostly angels are important as messengers or agents of God—communicating or implementing God's will in the world—and as manifestations of the glory of God. There is no prayer to angels in the New Testament, and worship of angels is expressly ruled out.

I have myself stressed the importance of angels in the scene of worship in heaven in Revelation 4. The whole of creation is here represented in heaven by angelic figures engaged in the continuous worship of God. The twenty four elders are, I think, the chief angels in charge of the cosmos, while the four living creatures, in the forms of a lion, an ox, a human, and an eagle, are the heavenly representatives of the various kinds of animate creatures on earth. They worship on behalf of all creatures, not just humans.

NOTES

1 MATTHEW 4 AND MARK 1. **2** LUKE 22. **3** JOHN 5. **4** JOHN 12. **5** LUKE 1. **6** LUKE 1. **7** MATTHEW 1.
8 LUKE 2. **9** MATTHEW 2. **10** MARK 16. **11** MATTHEW 28. **12** LUKE 24 AND JOHN 20. **13** ACTS 1.
14 EPHESIANS 2. **15** ACTS 5 AND ACTS 12. **16** ACTS 8. **17** ACTS 10. **18** ACTS 16. **19** ACTS 27.
20 EPHESIANS 1 AND HEBREWS 1. **21** PHILIPPIANS 2. **22** 1 THESSALONIANS 2 AND MATTHEW 13.
23 1 THESSALONIANS 3 AND 2 THESSALONIANS 1. **24** 1 CORINTHIANS 6. **25** LUKE 20.
26 COLOSSIANS 3. **27** 1 CORINTHIANS 15. **28** COLOSSIANS 1. **29** EPHESIANS 3. **30** 1 PETER 1.
31 EPHESIANS 5. **32** ROMANS 8. **33** HEBREWS 12. **34** REVELATION 2-3. **35** REVELATION 4-5.
36 REVELATION 8-10. **37** REVELATION 12. **38** REVELATION 13-14. **39** REVELATION 15-18.
40 REVELATION 19-20. **41** REVELATION 21-22.

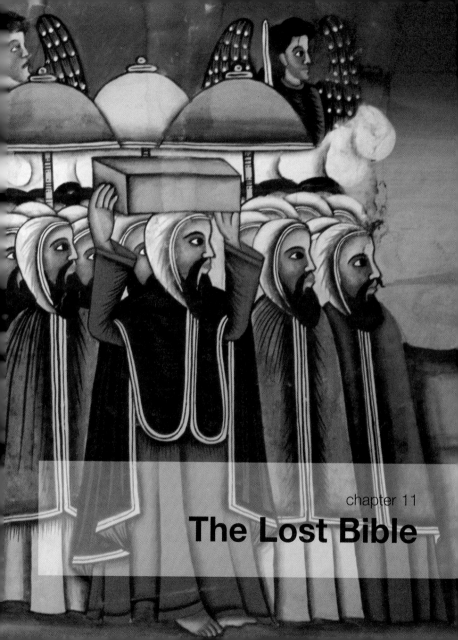

chapter 11

The Lost Bible

The Angel Life

After this my spirit was hidden,
and it ascended into the heavens,
and I saw the holy sons of God.
They were walking on flames of fire,
their garments were white,
and the light of the faces shone like snow.

1 ENOCH 71

When the Jerusalem temple was destroyed by the Romans in 70 C.E., the Scriptures were lost, but Ezra the scribe was inspired by God to restore them. The legend says he dictated ninety four books, twenty four to be freely available, but seventy only for the wise.[1] The public books were the Hebrew Scriptures, but the seventy must be other books from that time, which may even be as old as the biblical texts. One of these was 1 Enoch, which was Scripture for the first Christians, and which the Ethiopian Church kept in its Bible.

Altogether there are three Enoch books, full of information about angels. In the Bible, Enoch only appears in Genesis 5, described

previous page: **Procession with the Ark of the Covenant, Axum, c. 18th century, Ethiopian**
The ancient church in Ethiopia has preserved many early Christian writings and customs that have been forgotten elsewhere. They kept the important Book of Enoch in their Scriptures, and each January they still process with the Ark just as King David did when he brought the Ark to Jerusalem. Here, the Ark is carried at the head of a procession, and the two cherubim hover above it in a cloud.

enigmatically as a man who "walked with the *'elohim*, and then God took him." Did the writer of Genesis know the Enoch traditions, and simply allude to them? Or did later storytellers elaborate the mysterious lines in Genesis and invent the world of Enoch and the angels? We cannot answer that question with confidence, but if the writer of Genesis did know about Enoch walking with the *'elohim* and being changed into an angel, then this would mean that the angel world of Enoch underlies all the Hebrew Scriptures. In other words, the people who wrote the Hebrew Scriptures would have had their heads filled with angel images from Enoch, and would have believed that human beings could become angels. With the New Testament we can be certain, because Jude described Enoch as a prophet,[2] and the earliest Christian writers quoted 1 Enoch as Scripture. Enoch's angels were part of the early Christian world, and so the first Christians must have believed that people could become angels.

They knew that the angel world and the human world are not completely separated, as is sometimes said. A human being can become a heavenly being and then return as an angel on earth. This was the original meaning of resurrection—beginning the angel life before death, so that physical death was no longer anything to fear. This was a fundamental Christian belief, and so we can understand why the Church valued 1 Enoch, and why some people even thought it had been written by Christians, until pre-Christian fragments of it were found among the Dead Sea Scrolls.

A man of glorious appearance, dressed like a shepherd in a white goatskin, with a bag on his shoulder and carrying a staff. ... He said to me: "I have been sent by the most venerable angel to dwell with you for the rest of your life."

SHEPHERD OF HERMAS, VISION 5

right: **Angel on door of the Church of Debre Birhan Selassie, Ethiopia, 17th century**
Much angel lore was preserved only in the Ethiopian Church, and the traditions can help us rediscover the angel world of the first Christians.

following page: **Nativity and Adoration of the Magi, from the History and Miracles of the Blessed Virgin Mary (Tamra Maryam), 1721–30, Ethiopian**
This is further evidence that ancient traditions about angels survive in Ethiopia. Angels possessed great wisdom, and so an eighteenth-century artist has shown the Wise Men as angels.

Enoch's Angels

1 Enoch gives a full account of the "sons of God," the fallen angels who corrupted the earth. This is why Paul said the Christians were the new sons of God who would restore the creation.[3]

1 Enoch also describes Enoch's heavenly journeys, his vision of the fiery prison of the fallen angels, and how he went into the heavenly holy of holies. From this vantage point he looked out and saw the whole history of the world, which he wrote down as a curious animal fable. Angels were described as men, and mortals as animals. Some "animals" in his story were transformed into "men": Noah the bull and Moses the sheep both became "men," which means they were transformed into angels. Noah then built the ark, and Moses built the tabernacle—they accomplished great tasks which were God's will for the earth—so both must have been angels on earth. The Christians believed that John the Baptist was similarly an angel on earth.

In his vision, Enoch saw his own people handed over to the care of seventy guardian angels of foreign nations, described as shepherds, and these shepherds were cruel rulers. This was Enoch's way of saying that the Jews were subjected to foreign powers. When Jesus called himself "the good Shepherd,"[4] he was contrasting himself with these evil angel rulers. Some of these angels of foreign nations are described in Daniel 10 as "the Prince of Persia" and "the Prince of Greece." Enoch saw an angel scribe recording everything the shepherd angels did, as evidence against them on the Day of Judgment. The cruel shepherd angels and their followers were thrown into the abyss of fire. Jesus described this in his parable of the sheep and the goats—animals representing human beings—who were judged by the Son of Man and the angels. Some of them were condemned to the fire "prepared for the devil and his angels."[5]

2 Enoch, describes how Enoch was taken up through the heavens by the Archangel Gabriel and set before the throne, where he was anointed with oil of sweet myrrh by the Archangel Michael, and transformed into an angel. 3 Enoch describes how Enoch, transformed into Metatron the greatest angel, was enthroned in heaven where all creation bowed before him. This is exactly how Jesus is described in Philippians 2: exalted into heaven where he receives the homage of heaven and earth. The angel world of the Enoch books is very important for understanding New Testament.

And the Lord said to that man who was writing before him, one of those seven white ones: "Take those seventy shepherds to whom I delivered my sheep, who taking their own authority, slew more than I commanded them." I saw that they were all bound and they stood before him. The judgment was held first over the stars, and they were judged and found guilty and went to the place of condemnation, and there they were cast into an abyss full of fire and flames, and full of pillars of fire. And the seventy shepherds were judged and found guilty and they were cast into the fiery abyss.

1 ENOCH 90

He anointed me with his perfection And I became as one of those who are near him.

ODES OF SOLOMON 36

left: **St. John the Baptist as the Messenger Angel, with scenes from his life, icon, early 17th century, Russian**

John the Baptist was believed to be an angel on earth, just like other great figures in Israel's history. It was possible for a human to become an angel and for an angel to become human, or to fall even lower. The intermingling of the human and angelic worlds was a fundamental belief of the first Christians, who thought of themselves as angels on earth.

328

And I saw how he ascended into the seventh heaven, and all the righteous and all the angels praised him. And then I saw that he sat down at the right hand of that Great Glory, whose glory I told you I could not behold. And I saw that the Angel of the Holy Spirit sat on the left.

ASCENSION OF ISAIAH 11

left: **The Old Testament Trinity, icon, Andrei Rublev, c. 1410, Russian**
Angel lore is the root of Christian belief about the Trinity. The three "men," the angels who appeared to Abraham at Mamre have become a traditional way of representing the Trinity. The angels have identical faces, as they are all, in some sense, One. Here, the unity is further emphasized by the figures of the three angels forming a circle.

following page: **Jesus divides the sheep from the goats, mosaic in San Apollinare Nuovo, Ravenna, 6th century, Italian**
In His parable of the sheep and the goats, Jesus described how the Son of Man would return in glory with his angels and sit on His glorious throne. He would divide the nations as a shepherd separates sheep from goats. The sheep on his right would enter the Kingdom prepared for them, but the goats on his left would be sent to the fire prepared for the devil and his angels.

Angels in Early Christian Teaching

The angel of righteousness is delicate and modest, meek and gentle. When he comes into your heart he speaks to you at once of righteousness, purity, reverence, self control, of all good deeds and glorious virtue. When all these things come into your heart, you recognize that the angel of righteousness is with you.

But look at the works of the angel of wickedness. First of all, he is bad tempered, bitter, and foolish, and his deeds are evil. He casts down the servants of God. Whenever he comes into your heart, recognize him from his works.

SHEPHERD OF HERMAS, MANDATE 6.2

Early Christian writings show how the angel world of the Old Testament was preserved and adapted by the Church. Only the names changed. The Great Angel of Israel, the Lord, had already received the name Michael, and early Christian writings show that Michael and the Lord were still used in parallel: Michael and his angels fight against evil,[6] and the Lord and his angels fight against evil.[7] Gabriel and the Holy Spirit are another such pair. Then there are the seven archangels who are the sevenfold Presence, sometimes described as the seven spirits before the throne,[8] and sometimes as the seven-branched lamp, whose center stem was the Lord. Philo, the first-century C.E. Jewish philosopher, said the central branch of the seven-branched lamp symbolized the Lord,[9] and Christians still keep this image when they have three candles on either side of the cross on the altar.

Only fragments survive of The Prayer of Joseph, an important Hebrew text which showed that some great people had been angels come to earth, and that Jacob the ancestor of the Jews had been an archangel. Origen, the Christian scholar who died in 253 C.E., used it to explain how John the Baptist could have been the angel who proclaimed the coming of the Lord.[10]

The Shepherd of Hermas is a Christian text that shows the complexity of early Christian angel names. The Most Awesome Angel (God), sent a shepherd angel who is called the holy angel, the glorious angel, Michael, and the angel of the Lord. This glorious angel was very tall, and described as the Son of God. Hermas saw him in the midst of six other angels, so this was the sevenfold presence. In another vision, Hermas saw this angel of the Lord giving his people willow branches, crowns of palm, white robes, and seals. Then they all went into a tower, the traditional description of the holy of holies in the temple.[11] This had been John's vision too, but he used yet another name for the same angel: he saw the dawn angel marking the faithful on their foreheads with the seal of God, and then he saw a multitude before the heavenly throne, wearing white robes and carrying branches of palm.[12]

Contemporary with The Shepherd of Hermas is The Ascension of Isaiah, written by an early Christian prophet in Judea who used the pseudonym "Isaiah." He lived in a desert community with others who had visions of heaven, and in one vision foresaw the resurrection, and how the angel of the Holy Spirit and the Archangel Michael opened the tomb and carried Jesus out on their shoulders. In another vision, "Isaiah" was transported through the seven heavens by the glorious angel, who would not reveal his name. As he stood before the throne, "Isaiah" learned that the glorious angel was the Lord who would become Jesus when he came into the world. Then "Isaiah" was himself transformed into an angel. He described two great angels, the Lord and the angel of the Holy Spirit, worshiping the Great Glory. This was the Christian Trinity, described as three angels. The Great Glory was God the Father, and the two other angels were the Son and the Holy Spirit. He saw the Lord descend to earth to be born as a human child, and he saw the angel of the Holy Spirit tell Joseph about Mary's child. Then he saw the Lord return to heaven and take his place at the right of the Great Glory, while the angel of the Holy Spirit was enthroned on the left.

Only the section describing Good Friday and Easter survives from the Gospel of Peter. At dawn on Easter Sunday morning, the guards at Jesus' tomb saw the heavens open. Two very tall shining men came down, rolled the stone away from the tomb, and went in. When they came out, they were supporting a third man, who was also very tall, and a cross followed them.

The "Lost Bible" shows that early Christians thought of Jesus as the Lord, and the Holy Spirit as Gabriel. Christian prophets had visions of heaven and described their faith in terms of the great angels of Hebrew tradition. It was only later that they became known as the Holy Trinity.

NOTES

1 2 ESDRAS 14. **2** JUDE 14. **3** ROMANS 8. **4** JOHN 10. **5** MATTHEW 25. **6** REVELATION 12.
7 REVELATION 19. **8** REVELATION 4. **9** PHILO HEIR 215. **10** MALACHI 3.1. **11** HERMAS SIMILITUDE
8. **12** REVELATION 7.

chapter 12

Angels as Guardians

The Shepherds

Angels permeate and protect the whole cosmos, including nations, communities and individuals. St. Basil taught that some angels are appointed to nations, others as companions to faithful people, to act as their teachers and pastors. Angels also communicate by means of the people they have already taught, and so they in turn become heavenly messengers. Those they guide and protect extend the influence of the angels.

Guardian angels are often described as shepherds—they give pastoral care—but it is not clear in the ancient writings how shepherd angels relate to the other ranks. Perhaps the shepherds had a special concern for people, as individuals, as communities, and as nations. They were concerned with the affairs of human society and with the constant struggle between good and evil in the realm of the prince of this world. They taught people, and then gave strength and protection to those who had heeded their voices.

right: **The Archangel Michael on the Basilica of Nôtre Dame, Fourvière, Lyon, E. Millefaut, 1885, French**
Christians set up statues and icons as the visible sign of their heavenly Guardians. Here, a statue of the Archangel Michael keeps watch over the city of Lyon, just as an icon of the Mother of God stands at the entrance to Red Square to show that she protects the city of Moscow.

previous page: **Angels are near, 19th century illustration, British**
The guardian angels of children have always been an important part of Christian belief.

Guardians of Nations

When the Most High gave to the nations their inheritance,
When he separated the sons of men,
He fixed the bounds of the peoples,
According to the number of the sons of God

DEUTERONOMY 32

The Hebrew Scriptures mention the shepherd guardians of other nations, showing that they were not only concerned with the affairs of Israel. The vision of the Hebrew prophets and priests was not limited to their own land. The Hebrew Scriptures described some guardian angels as the "sons of God" who had been set over the nations of the earth.[1] Israel was entrusted to Yahweh, the Lord, showing that he was one of the sons of God. Enoch spoke of them as the seventy shepherd angels set over the nations,[2] and this is why the Lord is often described in the Hebrew Scriptures as a shepherd. King David sang "The Lord is my Shepherd,"[3] and Jesus described himself as the Good Shepherd, meaning that he was the Lord, the true guardian angel of Israel.[4]

Some of the shepherd angels rebelled against God, and failed in their duty as guardians; they did not protect the weak and afflicted. Their heavenly status had become worthless and Psalm 82 describes how they were thrown from heaven and punished with mortality. Enoch wrote about angel scribes who recorded the deeds of the wicked shepherd angels, so that they could be punished on the Day of Judgment.[5] Jesus taught about this in his parable of the sheep and the goats.[6] People who did not help the weak and afflicted, he said, were the angels of the devil, and Jesus the Good

Shepherd contrasted himself with the selfish and wicked ways of the other shepherds.[7]

Jeremiah described shepherds who came against Jerusalem with their flocks,[8] because the shepherd angel of each nation was present in its king. Conflicts between nations were seen as conflicts between their angels, and so the Lord punished Babylon by sending against her the spirit (that is, the angel) of the kings of the Medes.[9] When the future was revealed to Daniel, he learned that the Prince of the kingdom of Persia and the Prince of Greece, that is, the Guardian angels of those countries, would attack his people, and that the Archangel Michael would help his people to overcome them.[10] Enoch said that when Israel sinned, the shepherds of other nations were permitted to rule over them as punishment.[11]

The shepherd angels were an important part of early Christian belief. The shepherds at Bethlehem were said to be the guardian angels who were losing their battle against evil until the Lord himself came to earth to help them. At that time, the Romans were seen as the wicked foreign shepherd angels, and so when Jesus claimed to be the Good Shepherd, the true guardian of Israel, this was a political statement about liberation from Roman rule. Peter taught that each of the seventy nations of the world had a guardian angel, whom it regarded as its national god. Israel was privileged to have as its guardian the firstborn of the sons of God, and the Christians called him "Christ the god of Princes who is Judge of all."[12]

For every nation has an angel, to whom God has committed the government of that nation; and when one of these appears, although he be thought and called God by those over whom he presides, yet, being asked, he does not give such testimony to himself. For the Most High, who alone holds the power of all things, has divided all the nations of the earth into seventy two parts, and over these he has appointed angels as princes. But to the one among the archangels who is the greatest, was committed the government of those who, before all others, received the worship and knowledge of the Most High God.

CLEMENTINE RECOGNITIONS 2.42

left: **Tekla Haymanot and company of Angels and Archangels, c. 18th century, Ethiopian**
Tekla Haymanot was the twelfth-century monk who restored the ancient royal family in Ethiopia. Here he has joined the saints. The heavenly host are all dressed as Ethiopian priests, holding hand crosses and burning incense.

following page: **The Angel of the North, Gateshead, England, Antony Gormley, 1995–98, British**
The Angel of the North overlooks Gateshead like the guardian of the city. Made of steel from former steelworks, the Angel is a fitting symbol for a part of England that has felt itself neglected and has begun to seek its own regional government.

The Guardian of Israel

Yahweh, the Lord, was the guardian angel of Israel. As a mighty angel, he had many titles and names. In the oldest parts of the Hebrew Scriptures, the title is the Holy One of Israel, which means simply the angel of Israel. Thus, when Jacob blessed his grandsons, he prayed that the angel who had protected him, would also protect them.[13] In Jerusalem in the eighth century B.C.E., Isaiah spoke of the guardian as the Holy One of Israel, the Lord of Hosts—and the hosts were the angels. The guardian angel of Israel was the chief of all the angels.

In the Hebrew Scriptures we often read about the *angel* of the Lord, which meant the Lord himself in a visible form. The Lord brought Israel out of Egypt and led them through the desert, but elsewhere when the same story is told, we find that the angel of the Lord brought Israel out Egypt,[14] and the angel with the Name led them.[15] The Lord, the angel of the Lord, and the angel with the Name were different names for the same angel.

The guardian angel had to protect and defend his people, and so the Lord and his host were often described as warriors. The history of Israel is full of descriptions of these armed figures appearing in time of crisis. The Word—yet another name for the Lord—came from heaven with his great sword to liberate Israel from Egypt.[16] When Joshua was leading the Israelites into Canaan, he had a vision of the angel commander of the host of the Lord.[17] Elisha's servant saw heavenly chariots and horsemen prepared to defend Israel.[18] In the time of Jesus, the Dead Sea Scrolls community were confident that angels would fight with them against their enemies.[19] The first Christians shared this belief: St. John described guardian angels at the twelve gates of the heavenly Jerusalem,[20] and an army of angels ready to defend the city against the Romans.[21]

The guardian angels also protected against false teaching, with a sword as the symbol of true teaching. John saw the Lord in heaven with a sword in his mouth.[22] Jeremiah spoke of the guardian angels as watchers who recalled their people to right teaching.[23] There were watchers set on the walls of Jerusalem,[24] who sometimes failed and became "blind" shepherds because they had lost sight of true teaching.[25] The Angels of peace—another name for guardians— looked down and wept at the state of their land,[26] because as guardians they could not protect people who did not listen to them. This is why Jesus wept over Jerusalem and foresaw its destruction; the city did not recognize him when he came.[27]

In the bodiless world of angels, there is no gender distinction, and so the guardian angel of Israel was described sometimes as male, sometimes as female. Wisdom—the feminine name for the guardian— had received Israel as her heritage.[28] She had protected Adam, preserved Abraham, prospered Joseph, and guided Israel through the desert.[29] Isaiah used yet more of her many titles when he described her as the virgin daughter of Zion who scorned the Assyrian army threatening her city, and as the Holy One of Israel who drove them back.[30]

following page: **The Slaying of the Assyrians, James J. Tissot, 1896–1900, French**

People believed that nobody could capture Jerusalem because it was the city of the Lord and he defended it. In 701 B.C.E. an Assyrian army threatened the city and was destroyed by plague before it could attack. Isaiah said the army had been destroyed by the angel of the Lord.

The angels are the dispensers and administrators of the divine beneficence toward us. They regard our safety, undertake our defense, direct our ways, and exercise a constant solicitude that no evil befall us.

JOHN CALVIN, *INSTITUTES*

left: **St. Michael, the Archangel, Piero della Francesca, 1469, Italian**
The Archangel Michael was the patron angel of Israel, and his role often overlaps with that of the Lord. In the Book of Revelation the heavenly warrior who fights against evil is named as Michael and as the Word of God, the King of Kings, and Lord of Lords. Here, Michael has beheaded the serpent, the symbol of evil.

O Everlasting God who hast ordained and constituted the services of angels and men in wonderful order: mercifully grant that, as the holy angels always do thee service in heaven, so by thy appointment they may succour and defend us on earth; through Jesus Christ our Lord. Amen.

BOOK OF COMMON PRAYER COLLECT FOR ST. MICHAEL AND ALL ANGELS

right: **Angel Holding a Firearm, The Master of Calamarca, 1680,**
Latin American
One of a series of Guardian angels and Archangels painted in Bolivia in the mid-seventeenth century. They are dressed in the ceremonial uniform of the Spanish royal infantry and hold muskets.

In old days there were angels who came and took men by the hand and led them away from the city of destruction. We see no white-winged angels now. But yet men are led away from threatening destruction: a hand is put into theirs, which leads them forth gently towards a calm and bright land, so that they look no more backward; and the hand may be a little child's.

GEORGE ELIOT, *SILAS MARNER*

left: **Atom Man vs Superman, film poster, 1950, American**
Superman is a guardian angel figure, protecting the good and fighting against evil, a theme which also appeared in the *Star Wars* trilogy (1977, 1980, 1983). Many films have an angel character sent to earth, such as Clarence Oddbody, the apprentice guardian angel in *It's a Wonderful Life* (1946) or Billy Bigelow in *Carousel* (1956).

following page: **Scene from *A Matter of Life and Death*, 1946, directed by Michael Powell and Emeric Pressburger, British**
Wartime films often had a character return from heaven to help people cope with tragedy; during 1943 alone this was the theme of *Happy Land*, *The Human Comedy*, and *A Guy Named Joe*.

O welcome pure-eyed Faith, white handed Hope,
Thou hovering angel girt with golden wings.

JOHN MILTON, "COMUS, A MASK"

right: **"Nose art" on a World War II USAF airplane**
There are accounts of angels protecting pilots in battle. Air Chief Marshall Sir Hugh Dowding spoke about pilots in the Battle of Britain who had been helped by angels. Pilots in other aircraft had seen another figure in the cockpit when the pilot himself had been wounded or killed. Here, an angel with a tommy gun is painted on a U.S. fighter plane.

following page: **Mourning angels and airplanes on the ceiling of the Memorial, American Cemetery and Memorial, Madingley, Cambridgeshire, England, Francis Scott Bradford, 1956, American**

AIRMEN~WHO~HAD~GONE~BEFORE

EMORY~OF~THOSE~MEN~OF~THE~C

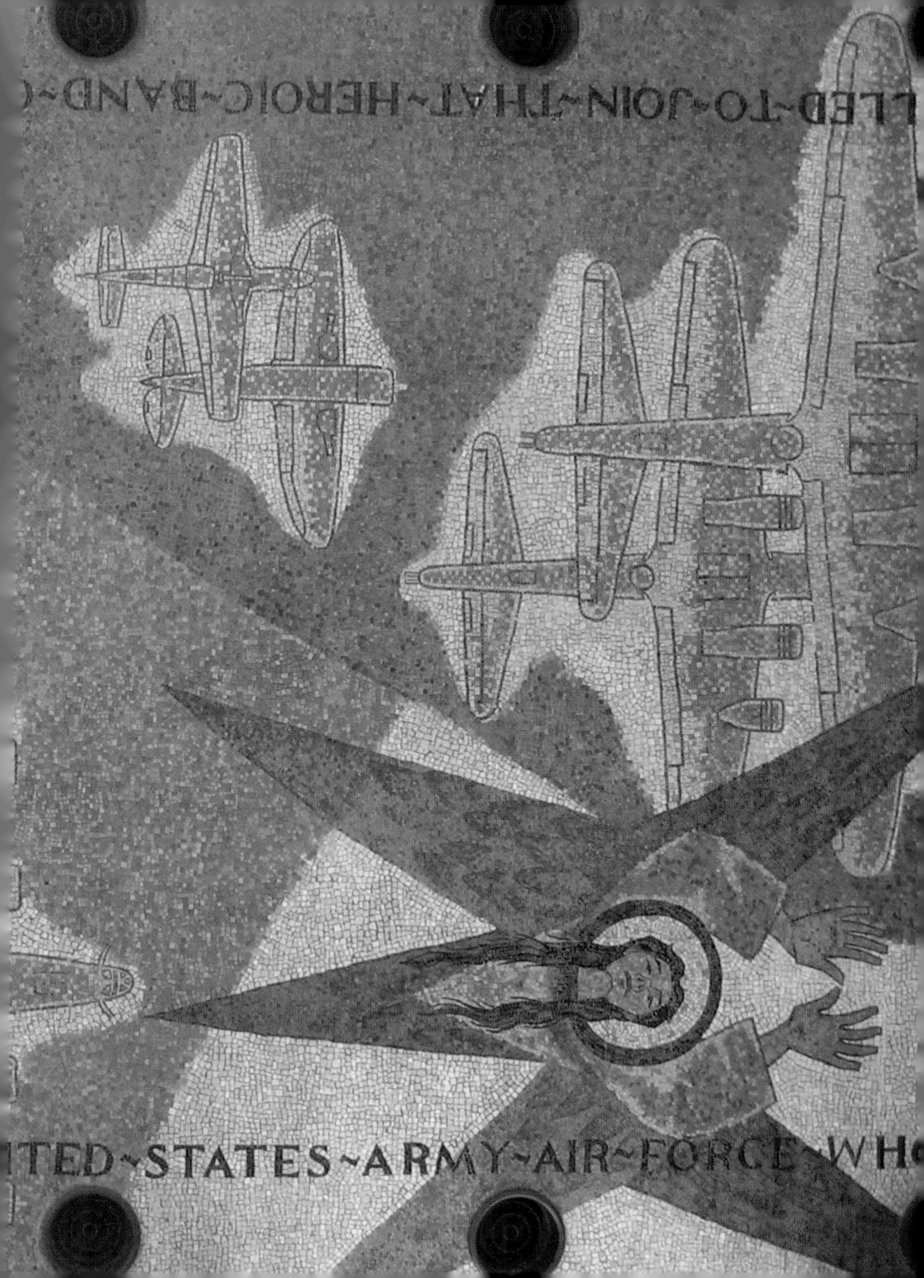
LLED~TO~JOIN~THAT~HEROIC~BAND~
ITED~STATES~ARMY~AIR~FORCE~WH

Guardians of Churches

St. John received messages from the heavenly Lord, and sent them as seven letters to the angels of the seven churches of Asia Minor.[31] The letters show what the earliest Christians believed about guardian angels. Through the prophets they received teaching from the Lord in heaven, and were assured of protection if they were faithful. The guardian angels here are the seven bishops, who were warned of the danger of false teaching and of imminent judgment if they persisted in error. The faithful would receive their reward in heaven, and have no need to fear tribulation. The Lord's Prayer reflects such a situation: "Lead us not into temptation"—of wrong teaching and lifestyle—"but deliver us from evil"—the promised protection for the faithful.

Ezekiel had warned the shepherds who failed in their duty that the Lord himself would come to seek out his people,[32] and the Greek version of Ezekiel 34 uses a word that explains the origin of the word "bishop," *episkopos*, "the one who seeks out." He is the shepherd angel of his flock: bishops in the Western Church carry the shepherd's crook and in the Eastern Church the serpent staff of a messenger. Ignatius, the martyr bishop of Antioch around 100 C.E. said a bishop was to be like God to his people.[33]

right: **Heliodorus driven from the Temple (detail), fresco in the Church of Gesu Nuovo, Naples, Francesco Solimena, 1725, Italian**
When Heliodorus the Syrian general attempted to rob the temple in Jerusalem (about 180 B.C.E.), three angel warriors appeared: one, identified as the Lord, was mounted on a magnificently caparisoned horse, and had armor and weapons of gold; the other two scourged the general until his men carried him away. Josephus said that heavenly armies were seen in the skies at sunset a few months before the temple was destroyed in 70 C.E.

An angel of Paradise, no less, is always beside me, wrapped in everlasting ecstasy on his Lord. So I am ever under the gaze of an angel who protects and prays for me.

POPE JOHN XXIII

left: **Papal crozier with the Virgin Mary and the Archangel Gabriel**
A bishop in the Western Church carries a crozier, a shepherd's crook, to show that he is the shepherd angel of his flock. The Pope's elaborate crozier depicts the Annunciation.

Guardian Angels

People have guardian angels. Jesus taught that everyone has an angel looking towards God, and they were shepherd angels. The parable of the lost sheep is part of Jesus' teaching about Guardian angels. He must have believed they were God's agents to bring back sinners from a path that would destroy them.[34]

The angels strengthened their charges against the forces of evil. The guardian angel was called a shepherd, a guard, a defender, and a helper. From the very beginning, Christian writings emphasized that there was a constant struggle between good and evil, between good teaching, which led toward an angel lifestyle, and bad teaching, the work of the great deceiver, which led to destruction. Sometimes it was difficult to know which was the evil voice. Angels of darkness could appear like angels of light, because they were deceivers. The guardian angel protected the faithful soul like an army, said St. Basil in the fourth century, unless he was driven away by sin, because he could not help those who did not heed his voice.

The angel struggle is glimpsed in the gospels. At his baptism, Jesus learned that he was the Son of God, but then the devil tempted him in the wilderness: "If you are the Son of God..." Then, says St. Luke, the devil left him until he had another opportunity.[35] When St. Peter tempted Jesus to avoid the way of suffering,[36] Jesus recognized the voice of Satan in his friend. St. John says that when Jesus had accepted the way of suffering, even the crowd heard the voice of an angel,[37] and during his agony in Gethsemane, Jesus was strengthened by an angel.[38] This was the guardian angel.

Everyone has a guardian angel from birth, but he has different responsibilities once that person is baptized. The guardian of the unbaptized person works through his natural reason, and so protects him from some evils that could harm both himself and others. Thus the power of demons is limited, even over those who have fallen under their influence. After his charge has been baptized, the guardian helps form the habit of good actions and is the inspiration of good thought, always leading the soul toward God. Since the guardian attends the prayers of his charge and takes them to God, he is sometimes called the angel of prayer.

He is known as the angel of repentance when he "turns" his charge away from sin. Enoch learned about the Archangel Phanuel whose name means the face/presence of God. Those who repented and saw the face or presence of God, had begun their heavenward journey.[39] This is why the high priests of Israel blessed the people with these words: May the Lord bless you and keep you

> May the Lord make his face/presence shine on you
> and be gracious unto you
> May the Lord lift up his face/presence upon you and
> give you peace.[40]

As the Angel of Peace, the guardian strengthens Israel against evil, because after death, the soul is received by the spirit it served on earth. There were two ways—the way of light and the way of darkness —and a person has to choose one or the other. Before baptism, the early Christians had to renounce the way of darkness, which included such things as arrogance, duplicity, sorcery, sodomy, abortion, and infanticide. With the angel of peace as guide, a person had no passion for material goods or the pleasures of this world. The angel travels with his charge, protecting him from external dangers and spiritual peril. Raphael protected Tobias on his journey, and also showed him how to drive away a demon.

Hermas, the early Christian prophet in Rome, shows what the Church of his time believed about guardian angels. His own guardian

angel appeared to him dressed as a shepherd, and reminded him of the fundamentals of Christian belief and lifestyle. Anyone who observed them faithfully, he said, would receive what the Lord had promised. His angel assured him that he had power over the devil, who fled from anyone who did not fear him. Hermas learned that there were two angels with every person, a good angel and an evil angel. The latter brought bad temper, bitterness, and despondency, but the good angel brought purity, gentleness, and peace.

Origen used Gospel stories to explain the role of the guardian angel. The Good Samaritan was a parable about the Lord saving the man who had fallen among evil powers. When he left him at the inn, he entrusted the man to the angel of the Church, to take care of him until the Lord returned.[41] When Jesus raised Lazarus from the dead, he came from his tomb wrapped in bandages and cloths, and Jesus told "them" to set him free—not the crowd or Lazarus' family, but the Guardian Angels. The born again were set free from their grave clothes by the angels.[42]

When people today speak of the presence of angels, it is usually the guardian angels. Testimonies to an angel presence in moments of physical or spiritual danger, in moments of sickness or grief, or in moments of joy and inspiration, are encounters with guardian angels. They bring moments of peace and tranquillity, and it is easy to identify those on whom the Lord has lifted up his presence. They look different.

left: **The Archangel Raphael and Tobias, Titian, 16th century, Italian**
Raphael was Tobias' guardian angel, traveling with him into the unknown and showing him how to protect himself from a demon. He was also the guardian of his father Tobit, had noted his good deeds, carried his prayers to heaven, and shown him how to cure his blindness.

I Dreamt a Dream! what can it mean?
And that I was a maiden Queen:
Guarded by an Angel mild:
Witless woe, was neer beguil'd!

And I wept both night and day
And he wip'd my tears away
And I wept both day and night
And hid from him my hearts delight

So he took his wings and fled:
Then the morn blush'd rosy red:
I dried my tears & arm'd my fears,
With ten thousand shields and spears.

Soon my Angel came again:
I was arm'd, he came in vain:
For the time of youth was fled
And grey hairs were on my head.

WILLIAM BLAKE, "THE ANGEL"

previous page: **Good and Evil Angels Struggling for the Possession of a Child, William Blake, late 18th century, English**
Christians have always believed that good and evil angels battle for their souls, and that the angel they serve in this life will be the one who takes them after death.

O, speak again, bright Angel, for thou art
As glorious to this night, being o'er my head,
As is a winged messenger of heaven
Unto the white-upturned wond'ring eyes
Of mortals, that fall back to gaze on him
When he bestrides the lazy-pacing clouds,
And sails upon the bosom of the air.

WILLIAM SHAKESPEARE, ROMEO & JULIET, ACT 2

previous page: **The Baptism (detail), Antonio Bellucci, 1689, Italian**
The guardian angel takes on a new role after a child has been baptized.

right: **The Wedding, Marc Chagall, 1918, Russian**
A good marriage is made in heaven, and here the guardian angel joins a couple together, to bring peace and love into their home. Here, the angel symbolizes the Shechinah (Divine presence) that according to Jewish tradition is present at a wedding.

Into Paradise may the angels escort you,
At your coming may the martyrs receive you
and lead you home into the holy city, Jerusalem.
May a choir of angels receive you,
And with Lazarus, no longer poor,
May everlasting rest be yours.

IN PARADISUM, THE END OF A REQUIEM MASS

right: **The Guardian Angel, Wilhelm von Kaulbach, 19th century, Germany**
When Jesus comforted those who were mourning the death of Jairus' daughter
he said: "She is not dead but sleeping." Here, the child is holding onto the
guardian angel as they fly to heaven. Is this a dead child in grave clothes with
the flowers left by mourners, or is it a sleeping child in night clothes kept safe by
the guardian angel? Perhaps we are not meant to know.

Interview with Professor Christopher Rowland

Dean Ireland's Professor of Exegesis of Holy Scripture, Oxford

How did the first Christians think of angels?

Ancient Jews and Christians had a strong sense of living in a universe where relationships with humans were not the only kind of relationships. What one saw with one's physical senses did not encompass everything there was, for angels and demons were such an important part of everyday life. Their effects, whether benign or evil, could be an important influence. Living in the Roman Empire involved more than the tangible web of politics and economics. There were bigger invisible forces in some sense lying behind, above, and beyond the imperial system, forces as effective and influential as the soldiers and officials who ruled the empire.

This way of looking at the world, so different from our own, is one in which angels played their part. For Jews and Christians, both the individual and the community might be assisted by guardian angels, who acted in the name of God to support and encourage (e.g. Revelation 2-3 or Daniel 12.1). They were "ministering spirits." They did not remove human free will (though some believed they could), for the angels in some sense represented and reflected the attitudes and behavior of the human actors, whether positive or negative.

Ancient people had a strong sense of living in the midst of powerful forces that far transcended the human or visible. The Letter to the Ephesians sees everyday life as wrestling with "principalities and powers." In this struggle, one might become part of a community of people seeking to serve God, a community linked to heaven and part of the communion of saints and angels. It was to be involved in a struggle against the powers of darkness in which humility before God and neighbor, goodness and love—all ethical qualities—and not magical manipulation were the tools of resistance, justice, and peace.

NOTES

1 DEUTERONOMY 32.8. **2** 1 ENOCH 89. **3** PSALM 23. **4** JOHN 10. **5** 1 ENOCH 90. **6** MATTHEW 25. **7** JOHN 10. **8** JEREMIAH 6 & 25. **9** JEREMIAH 51. **10** DANIEL 12. **11** 1 ENOCH 89. **12** CLEMENTINE RECOGNITIONS 2.42. **13** GENESIS 48. **14** JUDGES 2. **15** EXODUS 23. **16** WISDOM OF SOLOMON 18. **17** JOSHUA 5. **18** 2 KINGS 6. **19** WAR SCROLL XII. **20** REVELATION 21. **21** REVELATION 14. **22** REVELATION 1. **23** JEREMIAH 6. **24** ISAIAH 52 & 62. **25** ISAIAH 56. **26** ISAIAH 33. **27** LUKE 19. **28** BEN SIRA. **29** WISDOM OF SOLOMON 10. **30** ISAIAH 37. **31** REVELATION 2–3. **32** EZEKIEL 34. **33** MAGNESIANS 6. **34** MATTHEW 18. **35** LUKE 4. **36** MARK 8. **37** JOHN 12. **38** LUKE 22. **39** 1 ENOCH 40. **40** NUMBERS 6. **41** HOMILY 34 ON LUKE. **42** COMMENTARY ON JOHN 11

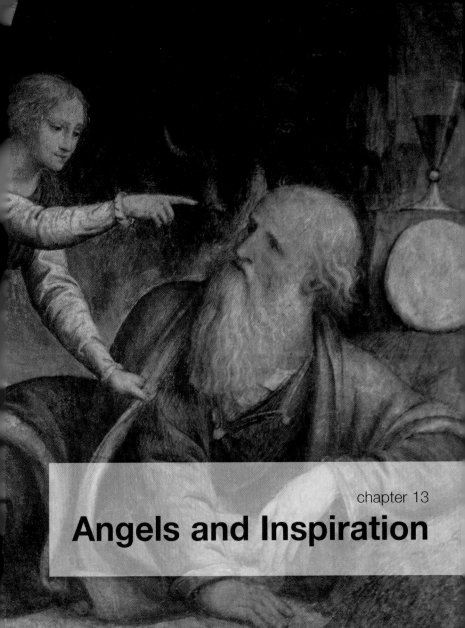

chapter 13

Angels and Inspiration

A New Creation

Generally, the germ of a future composition comes suddenly and unexpectedly... It would be vain to try to put into words that immeasurable sense of bliss which comes over me directly a new idea awakens in me and begins to assume a definite form. I forget everything and behave like a madman. Everything within me starts pulsing and quivering; hardly have I begun to sketch 'ere one thought follows another.

TCHAIKOVSKY, "LETTER TO FRAU VON MECK"

Inspiration enables creativity, so that people can make something completely new from the materials they have around them, whether they be physical objects, words, ideas, musical notes, colors, religious traditions—or whatever. Inspiration is revelation, and revelation is always compatible with what we can learn on our own, but it takes us beyond the fruit of our own efforts. Even those who have no place for angels in their worldview admit that their inspiration is given to them and comes from a source outside themselves, so that they see the familiar in a new way. They are conscious of an external source for their ideas.

Genesis 1 describes the process of creation; there is waste and void, and then the Spirit of the Elohim flutters over the water, and the creation begins to appear. Inspiration is a similar process; the Spirit comes to a person—that is what inspiration means—and something new appears. The angels bring this divine gift of creativity, and ancient texts show how angels enabled the creative process. More recent accounts of inspiration, which no longer acknowledge the angels, describe exactly similar processes.

Angels are the invisible powers, and the guardian angels link their charges to the invisible world, teaching and guiding. Philo, the Jewish philosopher who lived in the time of Jesus, said the invisible powers were bonds to hold the creation in being; they were knowledge, power, and a unity, and they were the Glory of God.[1] The angels bring what is needed to make sense of the world around us, and their inspiration enables people to join things together in new ways, to create new networks and patterns, to live as part of the totality of creation. Angels are themselves wise, transmitting light, love, and knowledge from God, the Source of all creation. They help people to build on the knowledge they have acquired by other means. At the lowest level, this may be no more than the simple process of linking together, helping us to see patterns. But this "discovering" brings fundamental insights on which the great systems of science can be built. All human knowledge is knowledge of God, and the angels transform it into Wisdom, by revealing how all things are one.

previous page: **Elijah Awakened by an Angel, Bernardino Luini, early 16th century, Italian**

Elijah fled into the desert to escape from Jezebel and her prophets of Baal. He fell asleep in deep depression, and was wakened by an angel who showed him bread and water to sustain him on his journey. There are other stories of angels sustaining travelers in the desert: Hagar and her son were shown water in the desert and survived, the Israelites were fed manna, the food of the angels. Such stories have a deeper meaning: angels bring sustenance in the desert of life, and enable the traveler to complete the journey.

Think, in mounting higher, the angels would press on us, and aspire to drop some golden orb of perfect song into our deep, dear silence.

ELIZABETH BARRETT BROWNING, "SONNET XXII"

left: **L'Art Céleste, Odilon Redon, 1894, French**

Many artists acknowledge that their inspiration is from an external source.
Here, a musician hears, and we assume writes down, music from heaven.

For God will deign
To visit oft the dwellings of just men
Delighted, and with frequent intercourse
Thither will send his winged Messengers
On errands of supernal grace.

JOHN MILTON, *PARADISE LOST*, BOOK 7

right: **Allegorical portrait of an Artist in her Studio, Michiel van Musscher, c.1680–85, Dutch**
Angelic inspiration flutters over any scene of creativity. What makes the finished work greater than its parts, and the work of an artist more than the materials with which s/he worked, is the inspiration that combined with the artist's skill to shape those materials.

following page: **The Prophet Jeremiah, Marc Chagall, 1968, Russian**
The prophetic writings were the result of threefold inspiration: the prophets themselves were inspired and even compelled to speak, their disciples were inspired to preserve and transmit their words, and later generations were inspired to interpret them.

Hearing Angels

Sometimes angels simply announce an event, and their unexpected appearance causes alarm. Messages of hope brought by angels— and by prophets in whom they had spoken—began with the words: "Fear not!" and were confirmed by a sign. Isaiah prophesied the birth of the royal child: "Fear not … The Virgin shall conceive…"[2] Gabriel spoke directly to Zechariah: "Fear not…" and promised the birth of John the Baptist. Gabriel spoke to Mary: "Fear not…" and promised the birth of Jesus.[3] An angel of the Lord spoke to the shepherds of Bethlehem: "Fear not" and told of the birth of the Messiah.[4] The angel on Easter morning said to the women "Fear not" and then showed them the empty tomb.[5] At other times angels warned of danger: in a dream the wise men were warned to return home by another route.[6] St. Joan of Arc was inspired by an angel to lead the armies of France, and the children at Fatima were visited by an angel before they saw their vision of Mary.

Revelation can come in dreams: Jacob saw the ladder of angels in his dream at Bethel,[7] and King Saul, losing his war against the Philistines complained that God no longer guided him by prophets or by dreams.[8] An angel of the Lord spoke to Joseph in dreams, telling him about Mary's child,[9] and warning him to flee to Egypt.[10] There is also a curious kind of sleep, "tardemah," in which revelation is given. Job's friend Eliphaz described the night vision and "tardemah" when a

right: **The Annunciation, Carlo di Braccesco, late 15th century, Italian**
Mary heard the angel and believed what she heard—that her child would be a son of God. It is impossible to estimate the influence that Mary's understanding of this experience had on her child and the way his self-understanding developed.

spirit came to him.[11] This was how people received warnings from God.[12] When Abraham had prepared animals for the covenant sacrifice, he fell into "tardemah" and heard the voice of the Lord promising the land to his descendants.[13] At the Transfiguration, the disciples saw the glory of the Lord as he stood with Moses and Elijah after they had awoken from sleep,[14] and the disciples were asleep in Gethsemane when the angel appeared to strengthen Jesus.[15] We do not know if Jesus told them later about the angel, or if the disciples had seen the angel in their "sleep."

Revelation often brings a sense of compulsion. Jeremiah did not want to be a prophet yet felt he had to pass on what had been revealed to him. It even caused him physical pain.[16] After his baptism, when he had heard a heavenly voice saying that he was the son of God, Jesus was "driven" into the desert by the Spirit.[17] For forty days he struggled with the meaning of that revelation—described as a conflict with the devil—and then angels came and ministered to him.[18]

left: **Joan of Arc having a vision, Jules Eugène Lenepveu, 1889, French**
In 1426, when she was a young girl, Joan of Arc heard heavenly voices inspiring her to save France. She was in the garden of her home at noon when she was aware of a great light and voices. She identified them as St. Michael, St. Catherine of Sinai, and St. Margaret, saints whose statues stood in her village church. They told her first to take the Dauphin to Rheims and have him crowned as Charles VII, and then to drive the English out of France. When sentenced to death by the English, she said, "I die for speaking the language of the angels."

Let us be silent that we may hear the whisper of God.

RALPH WALDO EMERSON

right: **Annunciation to Saint Joachim, Master of Berzenke, c.1540, Flemish**
The Infancy Gospel of James tell how St. Joachim grieved because he had no
child. An angel came and gave him the unexpected news that his wife Anna had
conceived at last. Their daughter was Mary, the mother of Jesus.

Dreaming over a subject is simply the faculty of allowing the will to focus the mind passively on the subject, so that it follows the trains of thought as they arise, stopping them only when unprofitable. Having learned to dream over the subject, the thinker must learn not to obtrude his own personal wishes, but to follow where the truth leads. He who wishes to express himself is on the wrong track: his aim should be to express beyond himself. In fact the procedure bears an analogy to the mystic way. The sinking of the personality; the retirement for the time being of the intellect from everything irrelevant; holding the intellect by the will so that it watches but does not disturb the natural development of the idea; merging himself into the great sea of life beyond himself in order that he may become one with it: these are the characteristics alike of mystic, seer, and thinker.

R. E. M. HARDING, *AN ANATOMY OF INSPIRATION*

left: **Jacob's Dream, Domenico Fetti, c. 1619, Italian**
Inspiration often comes through dreams or in the waking moment immediately after a dream. It can easily be lost. Here, Jacob dreams of a ladder between heaven and earth. He realizes that God is present even in a desert place, that wherever he travels the Lord is there, and that the presence of God is the gate of heaven.

Moving Pictures

Inspiration often involves thinking with images and pictures, and seeing them rearranged. The prophecies of Zechariah show this well. He was a priest, and knew about the furnishings of the old Jerusalem temple and the teachings of the ancient prophets. He knew the vision of Ezekiel, who had seen winged creatures take the Glory of the Lord from Jerusalem and carry it to Babylon. Zechariah had been concerned about his people's situation in Judaea; there was a famine, and the people returning from exile in Babylon had been exploiting the situation.[19] An angel spoke within him[20]—the literal translation of the Hebrew—and he was given a revelation for his own time based on familiar forms and Scriptures, but rearranged. He "saw" the ark of the covenant change from being a golden box holding the ten commandments into an ephah, the measure used for the grain, and it held a woman who symbolized wickedness. In his vision the female angels carrying the ark became creditors—the Hebrew words for women and creditors are the same—and he saw wickedness leaving Jerusalem and going back to Babylon whence it had come.[21]

The prophet Daniel found new significance in a familiar temple vision when an angel explained it to him. It was a night vision, so perhaps a dream. The high priest going with incense clouds into the

right: **St. Matthew the Evangelist, from the Ebbo Gospels, c. 820–30, French**

Matthew was inspired to compile his Gospel, blending the new message of Jesus with the traditions of Judaism, and so producing the most Jewish of the Gospels. He described himself as "a scribe trained for the kingdom, who brings out of his treasure what is old and what is new." Here, the angel fills his inkhorn and enables him to write.

holy of holies on the Day of Atonement answered the question that must have been troubling him: his people were being forced to worship a foreign king as a god, and what would happen to them? One of the angels in the vision explained that God would triumph, and his own people would overcome their enemies.[22] St. John had similar experiences; he saw the heavenly high priest emerging from the holy of holies on the Day of Atonement, but instead of bringing blood to cleanse and renew, he came as his sevenfold presence with bowls of wrath to judge the earth.[23] One of the angels spoke to John, explained what was happening, and showed him that the wicked city of Jerusalem was soon to be destroyed. These interpreting angels often appear in accounts of revelation.

In more recent times, people who made great discoveries in science have described the process of rearranging familiar things, of making a new connection—and of feeling that they had been given this as an inspiration. Sometimes this was in a dreamlike state, or even when they were asleep. The knowledge came from outside themselves and enabled them to solve a problem they had been investigating. The poet S. T. Coleridge wrote of the symbols that enable the human mind to contact the Imagination, his word for the Source of inspiration. The symbols, he said, were conductors between the human mind and the Imagination. Symbols are the way revelation is received.

1 Enoch incorporates an astronomy book that is a complex scientific treatise on the calendar.[24] We know from Greek writers that the ancient Jews were noted astronomers, and this book shows that they described their discoveries as revelations from an angel. The astronomy book has details of the movements of the sun and moon and stars, and says this was revealed by Uriel, the archangel in charge of the heavenly bodies. Enoch's astronomy book sets out a solar

calendar, with the sun rising through gates guarded by angels. The temple plan found among the Dead Sea Scrolls shows that the gates in the temple courts were positioned to mark where the sun rose on the longest and shortest days of the year and at the equinoxes. The calculations in the book are based on the sacred number seven, and so the system had not been imported from another culture. This was ancient Hebrew science, but the discoveries are recorded as the revelation of an angel.

Sometimes there are "signs"—everyday objects or incidents that become the channel for new ideas. Jeremiah saw an almond branch, and this became the inspiration for his prophetic message. He knew that the menorah in the temple was made like a golden almond tree, and that it represented the watching eyes of the Lord. He knew that the Hebrew words for "almond" and "watching" sounded almost the same. As he looked at the almond branch he had the revelation that the Lord was indeed watching his people, and that a terrible danger was imminent. Jeremiah had to warn his people of "the danger from the north."[25]

Inspiration was often described as transforming sense perceptions —anointing them—because to alter what we see we have to alter how we see it, and this is a gift of the angels. Eyes are opened, minds are changed, new things happen.

Sometimes it was not images but older traditions that were re-arranged and seen in a new way. When scholars detect "sources" and earlier material embedded in a biblical text, this suggests that an unknown seer had looked at familiar stories and been inspired to write them in a new way. Thus there are two versions of the history of Jerusalem in the Hebrew Scriptures: one written by the Deuteronomists,[26] and one written by the Chronicler.[27] These must have been huge undertakings, in effect rewriting the history of their people.

The process of rewriting—seeing the whole and rearranging the familiar—is clear in the Book of Jubilees, where an angel of the presence (re)writes for Moses the history of his people.[28]

There must have been a similar process underlying the Book of Revelation, where the prophet John recorded the visions of Jesus that had been explained to him by an angel.[29] This was a new revelation for the Christians. The prophet Muhammad received the Koran from Gabriel, and Joseph Smith received angelic revelations, which became the Scriptures of the Latter Day Saints. Both the Koran and the Mormon Scriptures have distinct similarities to the earlier Hebrew and Christian Scriptures, but in each case a new perspective was revealed.

right: **Joseph Smith's First Vision, Greg Olsen, 1998, American**
Joseph Smith, the prophet of the Latter Day Saints, received a vision during the spring of 1820. While praying in the woods, he saw a pillar of light over his head, in which were two bright and glorious figures, the Father and the Son. When he asked which of the many churches was the true church, he was told that they were all wrong, and so the Church of the Latter Day Saints was founded.

ولدم امیر المؤمنین علی المرتضى مسلمه اونده رسول خدمتن

Proclaim!
In the name
Of thy Lord and Cherisher,
Who created—

Created man, out of
A (mere) clot of
Congealed blood:

Proclaim! And thy Lord
Is Most Bountiful—

He Who taught
(The use of) the Pen—

Taught man that
Which he knew not.

KORAN SURA 96, GABRIEL'S WORDS TO MUHAMMAD

right: **The Archangel Gabriel inspires Muhammad, 16th century, Turkish**
The Archangel Gabriel told Muhammad to write the Koran. Here, in Muslim style,
the angels are depicted with crowns, and Muhammad has a halo of fire.

following page: **Visions of the Hereafter (detail): the Ascent to Heaven,
Hieronymus Bosch, 1500–04, Dutch**
Guardian angels take their charges through a dark tunnel into the light of
heaven. People today describe near death experiences in the same way.

Seeing the Whole

Certain people ascended into heaven—which means they entered the world of the angels. From this vantage point they could look back into the world of matter and time, and see it with the eyes of the angels. They saw it as a whole. The priests who wrote the hymns found among the Dead Sea Scrolls said they had stood in the assembly of the angels and acquired knowledge there.[30] Rabbi Ishmael, a Jewish mystic in the early second century C.E., also had this experience. He ascended to heaven, which he described as the holy of holies, and this meant that he passed beyond the veil of the temple. When he looked back, he saw the whole history of creation depicted on the veil.[31] Isaiah had had a similar experience in the eighth century B.C.E. The Lord rebuked him because he had forgotten what he had learned in the holy of holies, which he called "the beginning." Everything—all creation and all history—had been planned, and Isaiah had seen the whole and so seen the future.[32]

Writers and composers who have spoken of their creative work describe a similar process: that they have "seen" the work whole, and in the afterglow of inspiration have tried to set it down in conventional forms. Like the ancient prophets, they sometimes had difficulty in transferring the inspiration to everyday words, in recording—with whatever medium they used—what had been given to them. Ezekiel saw the vision of the chariot throne and heard a voice speaking to him, but his description is almost impossible to read. He used such phrases as: "with the appearance of," "like such and such," "the likeness of," and "as it were," showing that he was stretching language to its limits.

Losing the Vision

Aniconic cultures—those that forbid images—have to put their pictures into words. The Book of Revelation is complex theology which St. John saw as pictures but had to express in words. He described, for example, a Lamb with seven horns and seven eyes who took hold of a scroll and then sat on a throne surrounded by angels.[33] Without any context or explanation a picture of this curious animal would mean nothing, but expressing in words the theology it represents becomes clumsy and imprecise. The Lamb with seven horns and seven eyes was St. John's way of describing a human being—the Lamb—who was the sevenfold presence of the Lord—the seven eyes—transfigured by the pre-created light—the seven horns/beams of light. This Lamb had received the scroll of heavenly knowledge and been enthroned above all the ranks of angels. St. John had seen new pictures and, transcribed into words, they became an important element of Christian theology. Nobody supposes that he imagined Jesus as a woolly lamb in heaven. These were the symbols and pictures of the angel world.

More problematic for inspiration is the suppression of angels and imagery—the two go together. The Deuteronomists had no place for angels in their version of Israel's religion, they emphasized only the keeping of the Law and personal conduct. They forbade human access to the secret things—speculation about the holy of holies and

right: Birth of the Virgin Mary, Albrecht Altdorfer, c. 1525, German
The birth of Mary is here presented as the birth of Wisdom, with St. Anna's bed as the sanctuary or holy of holies. Here, the angels themselves are Wisdom's crown of stars. The artist has himself been inspired to combine the ancient images into a theological statement.

the world of angels. They were silent about temple music and everything it represented, and they denied that Moses had seen a vision of God on Sinai. They discouraged prophecy, accepting only prophecies that had already been fulfilled and dreams that did nothing to alter the status quo.[34] They were realists and rationalists, and religion was a private matter of rules, rewards, and punishments.

The Protestant world view is very similar and they found kindred spirits in the Deuteronomists. The predominance of Protestants in the formative years of biblical scholarship in Europe and North America has ensured that their worldview is now widely thought to be the Old Testament world view—emphasizing words rather than images—is now widely thought to be *the* biblical world view. With the Reformation in Europe, the mighty angels of the old Christian world became charming cherubs, the playful putti who frolic around the grand ceilings of Europe. Scientific rationalism abandoned angels, and so reduced religion to a private matter, severing the ancient links between human beings and the wider creation. The price has been great: fragmentation presented as freedom, and no sense of belonging or of purpose, beyond that of producing and consuming. Despite all this, great thinkers and innovators continued to recognize that the source of their creativity, their inspiration, lay outside themselves. They did not use the word angels—but they had entertained angels unawares.

left: **Rest on the Flight into Egypt (detail of cherubs), Anthony van Dyck, c. 1630, Flemish**
The mighty angels of ancient Christian tradition are here changed into the playful children of the Protestant world, the cherubs of popular imagination.

Interview with Professor John Welch

Brigham Young University, Utah

What do Mormons believe about angels?

For the Mormon Prophet Joseph Smith (1805–44), angels were almost commonplace, both in their frequency and in their personae. He described their glorious appearances and extended messages in vivid detail.

In September 1823, the angel Moroni made the first of more than a dozen visits to Joseph Smith. Of that occasion, he said that the angel stood in the air, his feet not touching the floor; he wore only a loose robe of exquisite whiteness and brilliance, with his bosom open. "His whole person was glorious beyond description, and his countenance truly like lightning," fearsome at first, but soon quite familiar. He addressed Joseph by name and announced that he was a messenger sent from the presence of God. Moroni stated his name and proceeded to give a detailed description of an ancient record that he personally had completed and buried 1400 years earlier. This angel then commissioned the young prophet to prepare to translate that record. He gave specific instructions, offering a variant version of a biblical passage from Malachi and interpreting a text from Joel, unfolding events that were soon to transpire. After delivering his message, Moroni left. The light in the room was all drawn back into his being, and instantly a conduit opened up into heaven, into which the angel ascended until he entirely disappeared.

Each September equinox until 1827, Moroni reappeared, restating and expanding his instruction. On other occasions, this same angel appeared to groups of three and of eight individuals along with Joseph Smith. These experiences were repeated and shared.

Other resurrected beings appeared to Joseph Smith and his scribe Oliver Cowdery in 1829. These angelic beings identified themselves as John the Baptist and as the apostles Peter, James, and John. In 1836, Moses and Elijah similarly appeared. They came to impart knowledge, to bestow keys and authority, to give comfort, assurance, and impressive guidance. All of these beings had tangible bodies in the ordinary form of human beings. Smith and Cowdery felt their hands placed upon their heads, which gave emphatically clear indications of the afterlife, of a literal resurrection, and of human apotheosis.

NOTES

1 ABRAHAM 1881 & SPECIAL LAWS 1.45. **2** ISAIAH 7. **3** LUKE 1. **4** LUKE 2. **5** MATTHEW 28. **6** MATTHEW 2. **7** GENESIS 28. **8** 1 SAMUEL 28. **9** MATTHEW 1. **10** MATTHEW 2. **11** JOB 4. **12** JOB 33. **13** GENESIS 15. **14** LUKE 9. **15** LUKE 22. **16** JEREMIAH 4 & 20. **17** MARK 1. **18** MATTHEW 4. **19** NEHEMIAH 5. **20** ZECHARIAH 1.9, 14, 19. **21** ZECHARIAH 5. **22** DANIEL 7. **23** REVELATION 15. **24** 1 ENOCH 72–82. **25** JEREMIAH 1.9, 14, 19. **26** 1 & 2 SAMUEL, 1 & 2 KINGS. **27** 1 & 2 CHRONICLES, EZRA, NEHEMIAH. **28** JUBILEES 1. **29** REVELATION 1. **30** HYMNS 10 & 12. **31** 3 ENOCH 45. **32** ISAIAH 40. **33** REVELATION 5. **34** DEUTERONOMY 13 & 18.

Biographies

Bishop Basil of Sergievo was born in Alexandria, Egypt and brought up in the USA. He is the spiritual leader of the Russian Orthodox Church in the British Isles.

Dr. Richard Bauckham is Bishop Wardlaw Professor in the University of St. Andrews, Scotland. He is a scholar of the New Testament and Historical theology.

Rabbi Geoffrey W. Dennis is rabbi of Congregation Kol Ami in Flower Mound, Texas, USA.

Dr. Bernhard Lang is a Roman Catholic priest and Professor of Religion in the University of Paderborn, Germany. He is a scholar of the Old Testament and of the Sociology of Religion.

Fr. Robert Murray is a scholar of Hebrew and Syriac, and a former President of the Society for Old Testament Study. He was born in China, and has taught for many years at Heythrop College in the University of London. He is a lifelong friend of the Tolkien family.

Philip Pullman is the author of the trilogy *His Dark Materials,* which has enjoyed worldwide success. In 1996 Philip Pullman was awarded the Carnegie Medal for Northern Lights. In 2002 he became the first ever children's author to win the prestigious Whitbread Prize for *The Amber Spyglass.*

Dr. Geoffrey Rowell is the Bishop who cares for Anglican chaplaincies from Madeira to Vladivostok, from Casablanca to Trondheim. He is an Emeritus Fellow of Keble College Oxford where he taught Church History, Historical Theology, and Spirituality for many years.

The Rev. Dr. C.C. Rowland is an Anglican clergyman who is Professor of New Testament in the University of Oxford, and has a special interest in South American Liberation Theology. He has served for many years on the board of Christian Aid.

Dr. Alan F. Segal is a distinguished Jewish scholar whose special interest is Judaism in the early years of the Common Era, especially the writings of the mystics, beliefs about the heavenly powers, and the similarities to early Christian thought. He has taught in Yale, Princeton and Toronto, and is presently Professor of Religion at Barnard College, Columbia University, New York.

Fr. Silouan was for ten years a monk of the Community of St John the Baptist, in Tolleshunt Knights, Essex, England, before moving to the Monastery of St. Anthony and St. Cuthbert in Gatten, Shropshire, England.

Professor John Welch is a bishop in the Church of Jesus Christ of Latter-day Saints. He is Robert K. Thomas Professor of Law at Brigham Young University, Provo, Utah, USA, and was the editor of *The Encyclopaedia of Mormonism*.

Glossary

amen: traditional ending for a Christian prayer, meaning "so be it."
Amon: title of Wisdom in the Old Testament Book of Proverbs, meaning "the one who joins together."
Ancient of Days: one of the names given to God in the Old Testament.
angel of the Holy Spirit: early Christian name for the Holy Spirit, imagined at that time to be an angel.
angel of the Lord, Angel of the Presence: the visible form of the Lord. Used to describe the Lord in the Hebew Scriptures.
Angel priest: can refer to human or angel. The priests in the Jerusalem temple thought of themselves as angels on earth, and of angels as priests in heaven.
angels of peace, prayer, repentance: all types of guardian angels.
aniconic cultures: cultures that do not allow the use of idols or images.
Annunciation: story of the angel Gabriel telling the Virgin Mary that she will have a son.
Apostles Creed: short summary of Christian belief, used from about 200 C.E.
arch fiends: greatest of the evil spiritual beings.
archons: invisible ruling powers.
ascension: ascending into heaven; usually used to describe the time when Jesus rose from earth to heaven.
Babylon: great city in ancient Mesopotamia; often used to describe any evil city.
B.C.E.: Before the Common Era, the period before the birth of Jesus.
Bodiless powers: angel beings who do not have a physical body.
Book of Jubilees: ancient book used in the time of Jesus, which tells the same stories as Genesis, the first book in the Bible.
Book of Revelation: last book of the Bible; a series of heavenly visions described by St. John.
Book of Tobit: book that most Christians have in the Old Testament, but that Protestants have in a separate collection of books called the Apocrypha.
bowls of wrath: sacred bowls used in a temple. St. John saw them in his vision, pouring the punishment of God onto the wicked earth.
Byzantine: anything connected with the ancient city of Byzantium in Turkey, now known as Istanbul, which for more than 1000 years was the center of the eastern part of the Church.
C.E.: the Common Era, way of reckoning time from the birth of Jesus.
***Celestial Hierarchy* of Dionysius:** book written by St. Dionysius about 500 C.E.

describing the different sorts of angels in heaven.

chariot throne: Jewish people in ancient times imagined the heavenly throne of God as a throne with wheels.

Chosen One: title for the Messiah.

circle of the living creatures: ring of four strange beings who surround the throne in heaven.

Cloud of Unknowing: medieval English book that describes the special way of knowing God that is different from the way we know earthly things.

consecrate: to make something holy, often a ritual using holy oil.

Council of Laodicea: assembly of bishops who met in Laodicea (now Latakia, Syria) some time after 343 C.E. and agreed on sixty new rules for the Church.

crozier: looks like a shepherd's crook. The staff carried by a bishop in the Western Church, symbolizes that he is the shepherd who cares for his people.

covenant: an agreement or rule.

Day of Atonement: *Yom Kippur*, the Jewish festival in the fall involving a day's abstinence from food and drink, and the offering of prayers of repentance.

Day of Judgment, Day of Vengeance: the time when the Lord will come from heaven to judge all living people for the way they have lived.

Day One: is the first state of the creation, before time or physical matter.

Dead Sea Scrolls: ancient books from the time of Jesus and even earlier, which were found in caves near the Dead Sea from 1947 onward.

Deceiver, Destroyer: names for the devil; Deceiver means "the one who does not tell the truth."

Deuteronomists: group of teachers important in Jerusalem from about 600 B.C.E. onward. They made many changes to the religion of Israel and wrote some parts of the Hebrew Scriptures.

diadem: crown.

divine throne: the throne of God in heaven.

diviner: a kind of prophet who attempts to see into the future using occult or supernatural means.

doxology: hymn praising God.

dawn angel: angel who appears with the rising sun.

elders: mysterious figures around the heavenly throne in the Book of Revelation.

Elijah figure: someone who looks and acts like Elijah, the Old Testament prophet who lived about 800 B.C.E.

'elohim: the Hebrew word for God. Unusually, it is a plural form, unlike other religions.

Enoch: ancient prophet. Many books of prophecies and visions are linked to him.

Ephah: measure for dry goods such as corn, used in ancient Jerusalem.

episkopos: Greek word for a bishop.

eternal covenant: rule or bond that keeps all of creation secure.

Eternal Holy One: the divine being who has no beginning and no end, who exists outside time.

Eucharist: the most important Christian service of worship, when people consume bread and wine; it means thanksgiving.

Evangelists: wrote the Gospels, the four books in the Bible, which tell about Jesus' life on earth.

Exodus: the story of Moses leading the Israelites out of Egypt where they had been slaves. The waters of the Red Sea parted to let them through.

exorcism: driving out evil spirits from either a place or person.

fiery throne: the throne of God, which was imagined as a place of fire.

firmament: the part of creation that separated heaven from earth, often imagined as the sky.

four-in-one: way of describing a heavenly being who is sometimes understood as being four distinct beings as well as only one who somehow includes all four.

Garden of God: an ancient way of imagining heaven, as a garden full of angels.

Glorious Angel: early Christian way of describing the greatest of the angels.

Glory, Glory of the Lord: radiant light associated with the presence of the Lord.

Gnosticism: religious system that flourished in the early years of Christianity and claimed to teach secret heavenly knowledge.

Good Shepherd: one of the titles given to Jesus, to show that he was the guardian shepherd angel of Israel.

Great Angel of Israel: the guardian angel of Israel, often called the Lord.

Great Glory, Great Holy One, Holy One: ways of describing the Great Angel of Israel.

Great Prince: way of describing one of the highest angels.

guardians: angels who protected people or places.

hashmal: Hebrew word whose exact meaning is not known, but which probably indicated a shining yellow color.

heart of the creation: invisible center of the whole world where God was believed to be.

heavenly harmony: both the music that angels sing and the sense of peace and wholeness that it represents.

heavenly host: all the angels in heaven.

heavenly household: way of describing heaven as the palace of a great king with all his servants.

heavenly sanctuary: the temple in heaven where the angels worshiped God.

heavenly throne: *see* chariot throne.

Hekhalot: Hebrew word meaning palaces, usually the heavenly palaces of God and the angels. Hekhalot texts are books that describe those palaces.

high priest: the most important priest in the temple in Jerusalem.

holy of holies: the most important holy place in a temple.

Holy One of Israel: guardian angel of Israel, see Great Glory.

holy ones, hosts: angels.

Holy Spirit: way of describing the power of God at work in human life and in the world.

Holy Wisdom: another way of describing the Holy Spirit, emphasizing the effect she has on the human mind.

host of heaven: see heavenly host.

icons: special pictures of saints and angels that are found in all Orthodox churches, now found in many other kinds of church too.

inspiration of Scripture: the holy writings were written after God had influenced the writer, thus making him or her write in a special way.

invisible creation: those parts of the creation we cannot normally see, but whose effects we can see. The angels are the invisible creation.

invocation: calling to God to come to us, often to help.

Ka'abah: the holy place in Mecca where Muslims go on pilgrimage.

king of Tyre: ruler of the ancient city of Tyre in modern-day Lebanon.

Koran: the sacred text of Islam.

Lamb, or Lamb of God: often used to describe Jesus.

Lesser Yahweh: title given to a mighty angel who was the representative of Yahweh, the Angel of Israel, *see* Yahweh.

Levites: lower rank of priests in the Jerusalem temple.

Light of the World: title given to Jesus to show that he and his teaching drive away the darkness of evil.

liturgy: the worship of God in a church service.

living creatures: *see* circle of the living creatures.

Logos, Logoi: literally word or words; describes the divine beings who make a link between God and humans, and teach them about God.

Lost Bible: name given to the ancient books not in the Bible, but that come from the same culture that help us understand the Bible better.

Mal'ak/Malach: Hebrew word for angel.

Malachi: prophet whose name means "my angel."

manna: miraculous food that the Israelites found each morning during their forty years in the desert. It was sometimes called the bread of angels.

martyrs: people who die for their faith.

menorah: seven-branched lamp in the Jerusalem temple, made to look like a golden almond tree.

mercy seat: piece of temple furniture in the holy of holies. It fitted over the top of the ark where the ten commandments were kept, decorated with a golden cherub at each end.

Merkavah: Hebrew word for chariot, *see* chariot throne.

Mesopotamia: ancient city in the region of modern-day Iraq.

Metatron: greatest of the angels. His name means "the one who shares the throne."

Midianites: descendants of Abraham and thus related to the Israelites. Midianites led the Israelites into idol worship and so Moses attacked them. The Midianites hired Balaam the prophet to curse the Israelites.

Midrash: the earliest Jewish interpretation of Scripture. The word means "seeking out" the meaning of a passage.

Mishnah: the collection of rules and regulations for Jewish life and worship, compiled about 200 C.E.

Moroni: angel who revealed the Mormon Scriptures to Joseph Smith.

Most Awesome Angel: early Christian title for the Great Angel of Israel.

Most High: one of the titles of God the Father in the Hebrew Scriptures.

motif: pattern that often appears.

mystics: people who have a different consciousness and come closer to God.

Nativity: the birth of Christ; the name given to the story of the birth of Jesus.

neo-Platonists: followers of the doctrines of the Greek philosopher Plato, originating in the third century C.E.

neuter: something that is classed as neither masculine nor feminine.

One who had the Name of the Lord: angel or high priest who was the Lord's representative. The high priest wore the Name of the Lord on his forehead as part of his formal dress.

Ophanim: Hebrew words meaning wheels.

Origen: Christian theologian who died in 253 C.E.

Orthodoxy: literally "right worship," is used to describe the Christianity of the Eastern Church.

Parables of Enoch: second section of the Ethiopic book of Enoch. They are three of Enoch's visions of heaven.

Phanuel: name of an archangel meaning face of God.

Philippians: book in the New Testament, St. Paul's letter to the Christians at Philippi.

Powers: divine forces in the creation, another name for angels.

pre-incarnation: time before Christ was born as a human child in Bethlehem.

Prince of Light: angel title found in the Dead Sea Scrolls, probably meaning the Guardian angel of Israel.

Prince of the Host: another title for the chief of angels.

Prophets: holy men inspired by God to be messengers from heaven.

Putti: angels depicted as babies or young children.

Queen of Heaven: title given in the Hebrew Scriptures to the goddess worshiped in Jerusalem during the seventh century B.C.E. She appears in the Book of Revelation as the Woman clothed with the sun who is the mother of the Messiah. This title is also given to Mary in the Christian faith.

resurrection: literally, rising again from the dead. It can signify the continuance of either physical or spiritual life.

Sabbath Songs: some of the hymns found among the Dead Sea Scrolls.

Sacred Name, Secret Name: the name of the Lord, Yahweh, which is never spoken because it is too holy.

seal: a stamp carved with letters or patterns used to sign one's name or to seal documents and containers. The high priest in the temple wore a seal bearing the Sacred Name. It was said that the seal of God had secured the whole creation.

Second Coming: the belief that Jesus would return from heaven.

seraph, plural seraphim: highest rank of angel, a fiery being with six wings.

seven-branched lamp: *see* menorah.

sevenfold presence: the complete presence of the Lord in all his aspects, often represented by the seven lamps of the menorah which gave one light, or by seven archangels.

seven heavens: the seven levels through which one had to ascend in order to reach the throne of God.

seven-in-one, seven spirits: another way of suggesting the sevenfold presence.

Sheol: shadowy place under the earth described in the Hebrew Scripture, where the dead waited for the Last Judgment.

shepherd angels: guardian angels who dressed like shepherds.

Shepherd of Hermas: collection of Christian prophecies, given to the prophet

Hermas by a shepherd angel in about 100 C.E.

Shining wheels: *see* ophannim.

Sinai: mountain where God gave Moses the Ten Commandments.

six-plus-one: the pattern of archangels in which three stand each side of the Great Angel but are in some way still a part of the one Great Angel.

song of the elders: hymn sung by the heavenly beings, *see* elders.

song of re-creation: angel song, imitated by people on earth, which renews and heals creation.

Songs of the Sabbath Sacrifice: *see* Sabbath songs.

Son of Man: title given to Jesus indicating both his human form and heavenly power.

sons of God: title given to Jesus and the mightiest angels, showing that they were heavenly children of God.

source of life: the state or place or person from which life comes.

Stigmata: these marks resemble the wounds Jesus received on the cross, they sometimes appear on the bodies of saints.

strings and superstrings: terms used by physicists to describe how matter is formed.

tabernacle: a tent, in the Hebrew Scriptures it refers to the worship tent built by Moses.

tardemah: Hebrew word denoting a form of sleep in which people have dreams or visions about God.

Te Deum laudamus: the opening line of a famous ancient Christian hymn, meaning "We praise you, O God."

Testament of Adam: early Christian book compiled from several older writings. Not in the Bible, it contains a lot of information about angels.

Testament of Amram: the words of Moses' father; one of the Dead Sea Scrolls.

Tetramorphs: literally four forms; the creatures with four faces seen by Ezekiel.

Theophany: God appearing in a vision.

Theurgy: working with supernatural beings—angels or demons—and using their power to achieve miracles or magic.

the tower: one of the names used to describe the holy of holies, the most sacred part of the temple in Jerusalem.

third heaven: the place to which St. Paul ascended in his vision, *see* seven heavens.

Three in One: often described as the Trinity, this is the fundamental Christian belief that God is known in three ways: as the Father, as the Son, and as the Spirit.

Thrice Holy Hymn: song of the angels first heard by Isaiah and repeated in Jewish and Christian worship ever since.

thrones: rank of angels, also known as the Ophanim.

Transfiguration: the moment when Jesus' disciples saw him shining with divine light. It can also mean the whole world transformed by divine light.

Tree of Life: sacred anointing oil came from this tree in the Garden of Eden. Adam and Eve should have eaten from this tree but chose the fruit of the forbidden tree and were expelled from Eden.

tribulation: severe trouble and distress.

unity: several things or people joined or combined into one.

unity of Day One, undivided kingdom: state before time and matter were created, when everything was one.

veil of the cosmic temple: separated heaven from earth just as the veil of the earthly temple separated the holy of holies from the rest of the temple.

vested angel high priest: means a human being or angel who is dressed in the special clothes, vestments, that are worn in the temple.

visible creation: the world that we can see all around us.

War Scroll: one of the Dead Sea Scrolls that describes a great battle between the angels of light and the forces of darkness.

watchers: angels who do not sleep, guarding the walls of Jerusalem.

Water of Life: flowing from the throne of God in heaven, out through the temple, and into the world, it renews life.

wheel within a wheel: an attempt to translate what Ezekiel the prophet wrote about the fiery throne of God. He seems to describe curious wheels, or perhaps they were great rings of light, *see* chariot throne.

white garment of life: apparel of angels or those who had become angels. It was made of linen, the symbol of eternal life.

Wisdom: one name for the female aspect of God. She illuminates the human mind and helps us to better understand creation.

Woman clothed with the Sun: *see* Queen of Heaven.

Wrath of God: not simply the anger of God, but what happens when people ignore God's laws and cause disaster in the creation, which then affects both them and others.

Yahweh: Name of the God of Israel which is never pronounced, meaning "the One who causes to be, the Creator." It is sometimes written as Jehovah. In traditional Bibles it is written as the LORD, as a sign of respect.

Picture Credits

Introduction p.2 powerstock/National Gallery of Art, Washington D.C.; p.6 (angel detail): **The Martyrs Valerian, Tiburtius and Cecilia, Orazio Gentileschi, c. 1620, Italian** © 1990, Photo Scala, Florence/Pinacoteca di Brera, Milan—courtesy of the Ministero Beni e le Attività Culturali; p.7 © Francis G Mayer/CORBIS/Musée du Louvre, Paris; pp.8–9 © Araldo de Luca/CORBIS; p.11 © 1990, Photo Scala, Florence/Church of Santa Maria della Pace, Rome; p.12 Mary Evans Picture Library; p.15 © 1992, Photo Scala, Florence/Musée des Tapiseries, Angers, France; p.17 Powerstock/Museo di San Marco, Florence; p.18 © 1990, Photo Scala, Florence/Galleria degli Uffizi, Florence—courtesy of the Ministero Beni e le Attività Culturali; p.21 © Photo Scala, Florence/ Art Resource/Smithsonian American Art Museum, Washington D.C.; p.23 Powerstock/State Hermitage Museum, St. Petersburg.

Chapter 1 pp.26–27 © 1990, Photo Scala, Florence/Galleria d'Arte Moderna, Rome—courtesy of the Ministero Beni e le Attività Culturali; p.28 Powerstock/Padua Cathedral, Italy; p.33 Powerstock; p.38 The Bridgeman Art Library/Stapleton Collection; p.39 © 1999, Topham Picturepoint; pp.34–35 © 1998, Photo Scala, Florence/St. Mark's Basilica, Venice; p.36 © Adam Woolfitt/CORBIS; p.41 © 2004, Mark Pelletier, www.markpelletierphotogaphy.com ; p.43 J & B Sawkill, www.jsprints-ink.co.uk

Chapter 2 pp.46–47 © National Gallery Collection—by kind permission of the Trustees of the National Gallery, London/CORBIS; p.51 © National Gallery Collection—by kind permission of the Trustees of the National Gallery, London; p.52 © Sandro Vannini/CORBIS; pp.54–55 © 2003, Photo Scala, Florence/Heritage Image Partnership/The British Library, London (Or.533 fol.34); p.56 © Historical Picture Archive/CORBIS/Cathedral of Limburg an der Lahn, Germany; p.59 © Burstein Collection/CORBIS/Fogg Art Museum, Harvard University Art Museums, Cambridge, Mass.; pp.60–61 © 1990, Photo Scala, Florence/Baptistery, Florence; p.65 © Archivo Iconographico S.A./CORBIS/Moldovita Monastery, Romania; p.69 (angel detail): **Christ in Glory, Domenico Ghirlandaio, 1492, Italian** Powerstock/Pinacoteca Comunale, Volterra, Italy.

Chapter 3 pp.70–71 © 1992, Photo Scala, Florence/Galleria Sabauda, Turin—courtesy of the Ministero Beni e le Attività Culturali; p.73 © 2004 Bente Arendrup, www.arildrosenkrantz.dk, photo: Jacob Termansen; p.77 The British Library, London (Add.11695 fol.112v-113); pp.78–79 © Burstein Collection/CORBIS; p.80 © 2003, Charles Walker/Topfoto; p.83 © 1997, Photo Scala Florence/ Pinacoteca di Brera, Milan—courtesy of the Ministero Beni e le Attività Culturali; p.84 © 1990, Photo Scala Florence/Church of San Vitale, Ravenna, Italy; p.85 The Art Archive/Museo Tridentino Arte Sacra, Trento, Italy/Dagli Orti; p. 87 The Bridgeman Art Library/ Musée du Petit Palais, Avignon, France; p.88 © Peter Shelton—courtesy of St Mary's Church, Westwood, Bradford-on-Avon, Wiltshire, England; p.91 Peter Willi/The Bridgeman Art Library; p.93 Topham Picturepoint/Heritage Image Partnership/The British Museum, London (OA 1963.4-20.01); pp.94–95 © 1990, Photo Scala, Florence/Museo di San Marco, Florence—courtesy of the Ministero Beni e le Attività Culturali; p.96 The Bridgeman Art Library/Birmingham Museums and Art Gallery, England; p.99 Powerstock; p.100 Staatsgalerie Stuttgart; p.103 © 1990, Photo Scala, Florence/Monreale Cathedral, Sicily; p.105 Roger Viollet/Rex Features/Musée des Beaux-Arts, Clermont Ferrard, France; p.106 © Peter Shelton—courtesy of Holy Trinity Church, Tansley, Derbyshire, England.

Chapter 4 pp.110–111 © 1990, Photo Scala, Florence/Biblioteca Laurenziana (Laurentian Library), Florence (Ms. Plut.1.56, c.14r)—courtesy of the Ministero Beni e le Attività Culturali; p.114

Powerstock/Church of Santa Cecilia in Trastevere, Rome; p.118 The Art Archive/Eileen Tweedy; p.119 © 1990, Photo Scala, Florence/Galleria Palatina di Palazzo Pitti, Florence—courtesy of the Ministero Beni e le Attività Culturali; p.120 © 2003, Photo Scala, Florence/Heritage Image Partnership/The British Library, London (Add.11635 fol.522); p.123 The Art Archive/Museo Nacional del Virreinato Tepotzotlàn, Mexico/Dagli Orti; p.124 The British Library, London (Add.11695 fol.240); p.127 © 2003 David Miles, www.davidmiles.net ; p.129 © 1990, Photo Scala, Florence/Memling Museum and St. John's Hospital, Bruges—courtesy Stedelijke Musea Brugge; p.132 Powerstock/Brooklyn Museum of Art, New York.

Chapter 5 pp.136–137 Powerstock; pp.140–141 © 1990, Photo Scala, Florence/Ospedale degli Innocenti, Florence; p.144 © Archivo Icongrafico, S.A./CORBIS; p.147 © Historical Picture Archive/CORBIS; p.148 © 1990, Photo Scala, Florence/Musée du Louvre, Paris; p.151 photo © Yuri Klitsenko; p.152 photo © Yuri Klitsenko; p.153 photo © Yuri Klitsenko.

Chapter 6 pp.156–157 © 1990, Photo Scala, Florence/Sanctuary of the Madonna dei Miracoli, Saronno, Italy; p.158 © 1996, Photo Scala, Florence/Musée d'Unterlinden, Colmar, France; p.161 Powerstock/National Gallery of Art, Washington D.C.; p.163 courtesy of the Victorian Spiritualists' Union Incorporated, Melbourne, Victoria, Australia; p.164 © 2003, Charles Walker/Topfoto; p.169 © Arte e Immagini srl/CORBIS; p.170 Powerstock/Koninklijk Museum voor Schone Kunsten, Antwerp; p.172–173 © National Gallery Collection—by kind permission of the Trustees of the National Gallery, London/CORBIS; p.175 © Photo Pierpont Morgan Library/Scala, Florence/Art Resource/The Pierpont Morgan Library, New York; p.176 © National Gallery Collection—by kind permission of the Trustees of the National Gallery, London/CORBIS; p.179 © James Amos/CORBIS; p.181 © 1996, Photo Scala, Florence/Galleria Nazionale dell'Umbria, Perugia, Italy—courtesy of the Ministero Beni e le Attività Culturali.

Chapter 7 pp.184–185 © 1990, Photo Scala, Florence/Pinacoteca, Vatican Museums, Rome; p.189 Powerstock/Sistine Chapel, Vatican Museums, Rome; p.190 photo © Yuri Klitsenko; p.193 © 2004, Photo Scala, Florence/Galleria degli Uffizi, Florence—courtesy of the Ministero Beni e le Attività Culturali; p.194 Powerstock/museum unknown; p.197 © 2003, Photo Scala, Florence/Heritage Image Partnership/The British Library, London (Add.11695 fol.147v); p.199 Powerstock/Musée du Petit Palais, Paris; p.200 The Art Archive/National Museum La Valletta, Malta/Dagli Orti; p.202 The Temple Gallery, London; p.205 (angel detail): **The Sacrifice of Isaac, Giambattista Tiepolo, 1726-28, Italian** Roger Viollet/Rex Features/Archbishop's Palace, Udine, Italy.

Chapter 8 pp.206–207 © 1990, Photo Scala, Florence/Musées Royaux des Beaux-Arts, Brussels; p.209 The Art Archive/Bodleian Library, Oxford (Douce 180 fol.34v); p.210 Mary Evans Picture Library; p.213 © Arte e Immagini srl/CORBIS; p.217 © Francis G. Mayer/CORBIS/Frick Collection, New York; p.218 © Bettmann/CORBIS; p.221 © Gianni Dagli Orti/CORBIS; p.225 Mary Evans Picture Library; p.226 The Bridgeman Art Library/The Stapleton Collection; p.229 The Art Archive/Victoria & Albert Museum, London/Graham Brandon; p.230 The Art Archive/Bodleian Library, Oxford (Douce 134 folio 98r); p.233 © 1990, Photo Scala, Florence/Church of San Francesco, Assisi, Italy; p.235 © Archivo Icongrafico, S.A./CORBIS.

Chapter 9 pp.238–239 The British Library, London (Sloane Ms.3173 fol.8v); p.243 The Art Archive/Museo Diocesano Bressanone, Italy/Dagli Orti; p.244 © 1990, Photo Scala, Florence/State Hermitage Museum, St. Petersburg; p.247 Powerstock/Musée du Petit Palais, Avignon, France; p.251 The Art Archive/British Museum, London/Eileen Tweedy; p.252 The Art Archive/Archbishop's Palace, Udine, Italy/Dagli Orti; p.255 Powerstock/Bass Museum of Art, Miami Beach, Florida; p.256 © Historical Picture Archive/CORBIS; p.258 © 1990, Photo Scala, Florence/Pomorskie Museum,

Gdansk, Poland; p.261 Powerstock/Jewish Museum, New York; p.262 © 1990, Photo Scala, Florence/Parish Church, Povo, Italy; p.265 The Bridgeman Art Library/Mallett and Sons Antiques Ltd., London; p.269 © 1990, Photo Scala, Florence/Sistine Chapel, Vatican Museums, Rome
Chapter 10 p.272–273 The Art Archive/Roger Cabal Collection/Dagli Orti; p.277 Powerstock/Brooklyn Museum of Art, New York; p.278 The Art Archive/Galleria Nazionale dell'Umbria, Perugia, Italy/Dagli Orti; p.281 The Art Archive/Museo de Zaragoza (Saragossa), Spain/Dagli Orti; p.282 Powerstock; p.285 © 1990, Photo Scala, Florence/Prato Cathedral, Italy; p.286 © National Gallery Collection—by kind permission of the Trustees of the National Gallery, London/CORBIS; p.288–289 Powerstock/Toledo Museum of Art, Toledo, Ohio; p.290 Powerstock/Scrovegni Chapel, Padua, Italy; p.293 © Araldo de Luca/CORBIS; p.294–295 © Christie's Images/CORBIS; p.296 The Bridgeman Art Library/Victoria & Albert Museum, London; p.299 Powerstock/Sansepolcro Cathedral, Italy; p.303 Roger Viollet/Rex Features/Museum of Fine Arts, Quimper, France; p.306 Mary Evans Picture Library; p.307–308 © Roger Wagner, www.rogerwagner.co.uk ; p.311 The Art Archive/Real Biblioteca de lo Escorial, Spain/Dagli Orti; p.312 © Archivo Iconografico, S.A./CORBIS/Biblioteca Nacional de España, Madrid.
Chapter 11 p.316–317 © Dave Bartruff/CORBIS; p.321 © Werner Forman/CORBIS; p.322–323 The British Library, London (Ms.Or.602 fol.168v); p.326 Powerstock/State Tretyakov Gallery, Moscow; p.328 © Archivo Iconografico, S.A./CORBIS/State Tretyakov Gallery, Moscow; p.330–331 The Art Archive/San Apollinare Nuovo, Ravenna, Italy/Dagli Orti; p.335 (angel detail): **The Ascension of Christ, Perugino, late 15th century, Italian** Powerstock/Sansepolcro Cathedral, Italy.
Chapter 12 pp.336–337 J & B Sawkill, www.jsprints-ink.co.uk ; p.339 Powerstock; p.342 © 2003, Topham Picturepoint; pp.344–345 © 2004, Graeme Peacock, www.graeme-peacock.com ; pp.348–349 Powerstock/The Jewish Museum, New York; p.350 © National Gallery Collection—by kind permission of the Trustees of the National Gallery, London/CORBIS; p.353 © Arte & Immagini srl/CORBIS/Church of Calamarca, La Paz, Bolivia; p.354 © Swim Ink/CORBIS; pp.356–357 courtesy British Film Institute Collections; p.359 © Bettmann/CORBIS; pp.360–361 © Wayne Boucher, www.cambridge2000.com —courtesy American Battle Monuments Commission, Arlington, Virginia; p.363 © Mimmo Jodice/CORBIS; p.364 © David Lees/CORBIS; p.368 © 1990, Photo Scala, Florence/Accademia, Venice—courtesy of the Ministero dei Beni e le Attività Culturali; pp.370–371 The Bridgeman Art Library/Cecil Higgins Art Gallery, Bedford, England; p.372 © Arte & Immagini srl/CORBIS; p.375 © 1998, Photo Scala, Florence/State Tretyakov Gallery, Moscow/ © ADAGP, Paris and DACS, London 2004; p.377 Powerstock/museum unknown.
Chapter 13 pp.380–381 Powerstock/museum unknown; p.384 © Burstein Collection/CORBIS; p.387 © North Carolina Museum of Art, Raleigh, N.C./CORBIS; pp.388–389 © 1990, Photo Scala, Florence/Private Collection, Saint-Paul-de-Vence, France/© ADAGP, Paris and DACS, London 2004; p.391 The Art Archive/Musée du Louvre, Paris/Dagli Orti; p.392 © Bettmann/CORBIS; p.395 © Archivo Iconografico, S.A./CORBIS; p.396 Powerstock/ Kunsthistorisches Museum, Vienna; p.399 The Art Archive/Bibliothèque Municipale Epernay, France (Ms.1 Fol.18v)/Dagli Orti; p.403 © 2004, Greg Olsen, by arrangement with Mill Pond Press Inc., Venice, Florida 34285, www.millpond.com ; p.404 The Art Archive/Turkish and Islamic Art Museum, Istanbul/Harper Collins Publishers; p.407 © 1997, Photo Scala, Florence/Doge's Palace, Venice; p.409 The Art Archive/Alte Pinakothek, Munich/Dalger Press; p.410 © Arte & Immagini srl/CORBIS/museum unknown.
As well as the library sources for the photographs, the editors and publishers have made every effort to acknowledge the museum/gallery collections of the original artworks illustrated. Any errors or omissions will be rectified in future editions.

Index

Entries in *italics* refer to works of art. Page references in *italics* refer to captions.

F

G

H

I

J